YOSHIMASA
AND THE
SILVER PAVILION

Asia Perspectives

Asia Perspectives
HISTORY, SOCIETY, AND CULTURE

A series of the East Asian Institute,
Columbia University,
published by Columbia University Press
Carol Gluck, Editor

*Comfort Women: Sexual Slavery in the
Japanese Military During World War II*
by Yoshimi Yoshiaki

*The World Turned Upside Down:
Medieval Japanese Society*
by Pierre François Souyri, tr. Käthe Roth

Donald Keene

YOSHIMASA
AND THE SILVER PAVILION

The Creation of the Soul of Japan

COLUMBIA UNIVERSITY PRESS

NEW YORK

Columbia University Press wishes to express its
appreciation for assistance given by the Weather-
head East Asian Institute Publications Program and
The Blakemore Foundation toward the costs of
reproducing the color illustrations in this book.

Columbia University Press
Publishers Since 1893
New York   Chichester, West Sussex

Frontispiece: The Ginkaku, or Silver Pavilion.
(Courtesy Jishō-ji, Kyoto; photograph by Akira
Nakata)

Library of Congress Cataloging-in-Publication Data
Keene, Donald
Yoshimasa and the Silver Pavilion : the creation of
the soul of Japan / Donald Keene.
p. cm. — (Asia perspectives)
Includes bibliographical references and index.
ISBN 0–231–13056–2 (ALK. PAPER)
1. Ashikaga, Yoshimasa, 1436–1490.
2. Shoguns—Biography.
3. Japan—History—Muromachi period, 1336–1573.
4. Ginkakuji (Kyoto, Japan)
I. Title. II. Series

DS865.A82K44   2003
952'023'092—dc21   2003053124

Columbia University Press books are printed on
permanent and durable acid-free paper.
Printed in the United States of America
c 10 9 8 7 6 5 4 3 2 1

To the memory of Shimanaka Hōji (1923–1997),
friend and publisher

CONTENTS

CHRONOLOGY

1408	Yoshimitsu dies. Yoshimochi assumes power
1423	Ashikaga Yoshikazu becomes shogun
1425	Yoshikazu dies. Yoshimochi resumes functions of shogun
1428	Yoshimochi dies
1429	Ashikaga Yoshinori becomes shogun
1441	Yoshinori is killed at house of Akamatsu Mitsusuke. His seven-year-old son, Ashikaga Yoshikatsu, succeeds him. Peasant uprisings and violence in the capital lead to the issuance of the first *tokusei* (cancellation of debt)
1443	Yoshikatsu dies. His younger brother, Ashikaga Yoshimasa, becomes head of the Ashikaga family
1445	Hosokawa Katsumoto is appointed *kanrei* (shogunal deputy)
1455	Yoshimasa marries Hino Tomiko
1458	Yoshimasa builds new Hana no gosho (Palace of Flowers)
1465	Tomiko gives birth to a son, Ashikaga Yoshihisa
1467	Ōnin no Ran (Ōnin War) breaks out at Kami Goryō Shrine in Kyoto. Rival forces are the Hosokawa and Yamana families
1473	Yoshimasa resigns as shogun in favor of his son, Yoshihisa
1477	Ōnin no Ran ends inconclusively
1481	Yoshimasa and Tomiko separate
1482	Construction begins on Higashiyama retreat, beginning the Higashiyama era
1485	Yoshimasa enters Buddhist orders as a Zen priest
1487	Completion of *kaisho*, the "meeting place" at Higashiyama retreat
1490	Yoshimasa dies
1493	Completion of Ginkaku (Silver Pavilion)

Only the first ten shoguns of the Ashikaga family appear in this genealogical chart. The dates indicate the years when a shogun reigned, not those of his birth and death. The numbers indicate the order of succession. Yoshimochi, who had abdicated in favor of his son, Yoshikazu, resumed the functions but not the title of the shogun from 1425 to 1428, following Yoshikazu's death. Yoshimi did not serve as shogun, but his son Yoshitane succeeded as the tenth shogun.

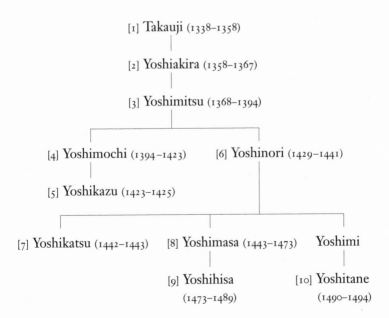

[1] Takauji (1338–1358)

[2] Yoshiakira (1358–1367)

[3] Yoshimitsu (1368–1394)

[4] Yoshimochi (1394–1423)   [6] Yoshinori (1429–1441)

[5] Yoshikazu (1423–1425)

[7] Yoshikatsu (1442–1443)   [8] Yoshimasa (1443–1473)   Yoshimi

[9] Yoshihisa (1473–1489)   [10] Yoshitane (1490–1494)

YOSHIMASA
AND THE
SILVER PAVILION

In 1953 when I was first living in Kyoto, I often went to a nearby temple, Tōji-in, in order to escape the din of the children in the school next door. The temple was virtually deserted in those days. I never saw a priest, though I was told that one came every week from the Tenryū-ji, a temple of the same branch of Zen. The only persons I ever encountered in the temple were a few young men studying for their university entrance examinations. The temple was neglected. Tall weeds sprouted from the roofs of the gates and temple buildings, and the *fusuma-e*, the paintings on the sliding doors between the rooms, said to be the work of the celebrated Kanō Sanraku, were smudged and torn, especially around the metal fittings. I don't recall ever seeing a visitor, though even in those days the celebrated stone and sand garden of the nearby Ryōan-ji attracted a constant stream of tourists, both Japanese and foreign. The Tōji-in was an ideal place to study without noise or other interruption.

Apart from the main buildings, the temple includes a small, curving pond in the shape of the character *kokoro*. Similar ponds are found in the precincts of other Zen temples, perhaps because the use of the mind—one of the meanings of *kokoro*—is especially important in Zen Buddhism.

Tōji-in was originally founded in the fourteenth century at the foot of Mount Kinugasa, in fulfillment of a vow made by Ashikaga Takauji (1305–1358), the first of the Ashikaga shoguns. His inconspicuous stone gravestone in the temple's garden is hardly of the magnificence one might expect of the tomb of the man who founded the dynasty of shoguns who ruled Japan from the fourteenth to the sixteenth century. Indeed, there could be no greater contrast to the elaborate mausoleum erected in memory of the founder of the next dynasty of shoguns, Tokugawa Ieyasu (1543–1616).

In recent years, an effort has been made to increase Tōji-in's appeal as a tourist attraction. The pond, and indeed the whole temple—buildings, gardens, and walls—look far better today than they did when I first knew them, though I remember nostalgically the poetic neglect. The interior of the main building has been refurbished; the *fusuma-e* are now protected by glass; and a much larger area of garden than I had seen before has been opened to the public. Picture postcards on sale in the temple attest to the beauty of its seasonal flowers and leaves, but I have no recollection of any flowers or colored leaves fifty years ago. For that matter, I even have difficulty in associating picture postcards with the gloomy presence of the Ashikaga shoguns. One small building, however, remains exactly as I remember it from the past: the Reikō-den, the hall where the Ashikaga shoguns are enshrined.

In one of the first articles I wrote in Japanese, I described this building, which had made a powerful impression on me, and said that it was cold even during the torrid Kyoto summer. Probably I was consciously exaggerating, but on a recent visit I definitely felt an uncomfortable chill emanating from the life-size wooden statues ranged on both sides of the hall. The glass eyes of these statues are their most disquieting feature, each face staring past the visitors with unblinking eyes that glow in the dim light inside. Their gaze seems to traverse the centuries, unwavering and unforgetting.

Before coming to Japan, I knew the names of three Ashikaga shoguns: Takauji, Yoshimitsu, and Yoshimasa. I disliked Takauji for what I interpreted as his betrayal of the cause of Go-Daigo, an emperor whose ill-fated struggle to retain his throne gave him a tragic appeal, at least to a romanticist like myself.

I was much more favorably disposed toward Ashikaga Yoshimitsu (1358–1408), the third shogun, because he was the great patron of Zeami and the nō theater. I knew Yoshimitsu's name also because of the letters he sent to the Chinese court. His readiness to accept the title of King of Japan, bestowed on him by the Chinese and signifying that they considered him to be a loyal vassal, earned Yoshimitsu the hatred of those who, believing in the divine ancestry of the Japanese emperors, could not tolerate servility toward a foreign country.

Hatred of Yoshimitsu was especially strong during the years immediately before the Meiji Restoration of 1868, which had as one of its professed goals the return of secular authority to the emperor. In the second month of the third year of Bunkyū (1863), nine men, followers of the Shinto zealot Hirata Atsutane, broke into the Tōji-in and removed the heads of the statues of the first three Ashikaga shoguns: Takauji, Yoshiakira, and Yoshimitsu. They then exposed the heads on the bank of the Kamo River, following the common practice at this time of "patriots" exposing for all to see the heads of men accused of being traitors. Beside the heads of the three shoguns, placards were set up enumerating the crimes of each. Yoshimitsu's acceptance of the title of King of Japan made him the worst traitor of all.

The heads had been restored to the statues long before I saw them. Of the three, Yoshimitsu's produced the most powerful impression on me. His mouth is turned down in a disdainful frown and his eyes glare, making him look more like an arrogant despot than a sensitive and generous patron of nō. This is not surprising. Although he was genuinely devoted to the arts, Yoshimitsu was one of the most powerful men of Japanese history: the de facto ruler of the whole country after he reunited in 1392 the two courts into which it had been divided for sixty years, each presided over by an emperor. Some scholars believe that Yoshimitsu's ambitions went beyond the office of shogun and that he planned to assume the title of emperor himself.[1] After Yoshimitsu entered Buddhist orders, he was accorded the title of cloistered sovereign (*hōō*), and in 1400, after his death, he received the title of *dajō tennō* (retired emperor).

Yoshimitsu's reign marked the high point in the political fortunes of the Ashikaga shoguns. He ruled without interference from other military lords or from the emperor, the sacredness of whose person was barely acknowledged. The nobles of the court aristocracy fawned on Yoshimitsu despite the repugnance many felt for someone not of their class; they were aware that they had no choice but to obey.

The shoguns' dominance over the country ended in 1441 with the assassination of Ashikaga Yoshinori, the sixth shogun, and during the reigns of his successors, the shoguns' power steadily eroded. When visiting the Reikō-den, I often stopped before the statue of Yoshinori's son, the seventh shogun, Ashikaga Yoshikatsu (1434–1443). The face and size of the statue make it clear that Yoshikatsu was still a child when he joined the company of deceased shoguns, but like the other shoguns he stares straight ahead, a baton of office (*shaku*) grasped in his right hand, youthful but by no means childish. I guessed (without bothering to confirm it) that he had been poisoned by someone who desired his office, perhaps a wicked uncle, but as I later learned, Yoshikatsu died of illness.

The statue of Yoshikatsu's younger brother Ashikaga Yoshimasa

(1436–1490), the eighth shogun, did not attract my attention, though his face—eyes close together and a small, weak mouth—distinguishes him somewhat from other members of the Ashikaga family. His skimpy beard contrasts especially with Yoshimitsu's flowing whiskers, as if to indicate that he belonged to a lesser generation. Not for many years did I learn that despite Yoshimasa's unprepossessing appearance and his many faults as a shogun, husband, and father, he contributed more to Japanese culture than did any other Ashikaga shogun or, it might be argued, anyone else who ever ruled over Japan.

Yoshimasa is remembered by most people as the builder of the Ginkaku-ji, the Temple of the Silver Pavilion, and (unfavorably) as the shogun at the time of the Ōnin War (1467–1477). Following that war, the authority of the shogun all but disappeared, replaced by the rule of provincial military governors (*shugo daimyō*).[2] In a letter to his son written in 1482, the hapless Yoshimasa complained, "The daimyo do as they please and do not follow orders. That means there can be no government."[3] Unable to assert his authority over the daimyos, he turned his back on politics and devoted himself instead to his quest for beauty.

The portrait statues of the Ashikaga shoguns[4] in the Tōji-in are not outstanding as sculpture, but they form an imposing, even fearsome, ensemble. The sculptor (or probably many sculptors) is unknown, but the statues seem to date from the early seventeenth century. The oppressively gloomy atmosphere engendered by their dusty ranks seems to confirm the impression that most Japanese have of the medieval period of their history. There are no cheerful anecdotes about the Ashikaga shoguns.

During my stay in Kyoto, I visited almost all the famous temples. At many of them, I was informed that the original buildings, of the greatest splendor, had gone up in flames during the Ōnin War. Hardly a building in the capital escaped destruction. Reading accounts of the desolation left in the wake of the warfare might make one suppose that the capital—for long the only major site of culture in the whole country—had been turned into a wasteland, barren as Carthage is today, but in fact the city rose phoenix-like from its ashes. A new culture, which had originated at Yoshimasa's mountain retreat in the Higashiyama (Eastern Mountains) area of Kyoto, gave its name to the Higashiyama period (1483–1490) and greatly influenced all subsequent Japanese culture.

During the Ōnin War, Yoshimasa continued to reside in his palace, even though it was situated no more than a few hundred yards from the worst of the fighting. He seems to have spent most of his time admiring his garden and his collection of Chinese paintings. His indifference to the fighting and the suffering it caused may have been exaggerated by chroniclers of the time, but there is no reason to doubt that Yoshimasa, having decided not to participate in the warfare (though as shogun, the supreme military commander, he should have led his troops), devoted himself almost exclusively to aesthetic pleasures.

The Ōnin War led not only to the birth of a new culture but also to the immediate diffusion of culture to the provinces. Poets, painters, and others fled the capital, where almost all the fighting occurred, to take refuge with local potentates. The poets introduced to their often barely literate hosts the literary masterpieces of the past, including the tenth-century anthology of poetry *Kokinshū* and the eleventh-century novel *The Tale of Genji*, and they taught their hosts how to compose poetry. Even the most barbarous warlord desired the trappings of culture that would enable him to feel like a civilized man.

Above all, the refugee poets taught their hosts how to compose *renga* (linked verse), the most popular variety of poetry at the time. *Renga* appealed to the provincial lords not only because it was largely free of the tedious conventions of the *waka*, the classic verse form, but also because it was flattering to compose poetry with a master from the capital, adding one's contributions to the "chain" of linked verse.

A *renga* sequence was normally composed by three or more participants who took turns supplying alternating verses in seventeen and fourteen syllables. Each poet was free to change the direction of the sequence as he saw fit. It was not considered desirable to create the impression that one poet had composed the entire sequence of a hundred or a thousand "links," but ultimately each participant was sharing in the experience of creating one long poem.

The rules of *renga*, at least when composed by professionals, were no less demanding than those of *waka*. However arbitrary they may seem today, these rules had a literary grounding, but the provincial lords who participated in *renga* sessions probably thought of them as no more than part of an elaborate game. If they could not memorize the rules, their teachers were ready to call attention to infractions. The daimyos enjoyed *renga* sessions so much that they offered visiting poets months or even years of hospitality.

Renga were composed through the worst of the Ōnin War. In fact, this was the golden age of *renga*, perhaps because at a time of destruction and death, composing the linked verses provided occasions for bringing people together to share with friends the pleasure of creating poems. Today the composition of *renga* is no longer of much interest except to a handful of scholars, but the idea of several people composing an extended poem—whether or not in keeping with rules—has in recent years found exponents even outside Japan, and *haiku*, which originally was the first link in a chain of *renga*, rank today as the most popular of all Japanese verse forms.

Poems in Chinese (*kanshi*), mainly composed by Zen monks, were of major literary importance during the Higashiyama period. For a long time, such poems were dismissed by historians of Japanese literature as mere imitations of Chinese examples, but their importance has been rediscovered in recent years. Of particular interest are the Chinese poems of Ikkyū Sōjun (1394–1481), a memorably eccentric Zen monk. In contrast, those Buddhist priests who were concerned more with proselytization than with poetry found fertile ground at this time of warfare and death for sowing the seeds of faith. Rennyo (1415–1499) was known especially for his epistles (*ofumi*) in which he used simple language to explain the essence of salvation through faith in Amida Buddha. The sect of Buddhism he founded, True Pure Land (Jōdo shinshū), became the religion of the Japanese masses.

The nō theater also flourished. Although Zeami, the supreme master of the art, died before the Higashiyama period, his successors frequently performed for Yoshimasa. The austere expression of the nō plays was congenial to the Higashiyama taste. Masks made during this period rank as the finest and are used to this day, and the robes bestowed on actors by Yoshimasa after outstanding performances are treasured and still serve as models for new robes.

The bare nō stage itself was a perfect example of the evocative simplicity that had become an aesthetic ideal. An even more typical form of architecture invented during the Higashiyama period, the *shoin-zukuri*, developed into the most common variety of traditional Japanese houses. Likewise, the gardens surrounding the buildings provided models for the gardens of later centuries.

Many painters, headed by the great Sesshū (1420–1506), were active in both the capital and the provinces. Their most characteristic works were ink paintings (*suibokuga*), then enjoying a vogue in China, rather than the brightly colored scrolls of earlier times, a further expression of the preference for simplicity and suggestion.

The tea ceremony (*chanoyu*), another important development in Higashiyama culture, originated in a small room at the Ginkaku-ji where Yoshimasa offered tea to his friends. Today, a tiny wooden ladle (*chashaku*), even if it is hardly more than a bent piece of bamboo, may be worth a fortune if a connection with Yoshimasa can be established. Most of the tea bowls used in the ceremony today are simpler and sturdier than the Chinese ceramics that Yoshimasa himself preferred, but they harmonize even better with the bare interiors of the rooms where he first drank tea with his friends. Flower arrangement developed along with the tea ceremony, enhancing the rooms with the beauty and spiritual qualities of blossoms artistically arranged in ceramic vases.

The soul (*kokoro*) of Japan, the aesthetic preferences of the Japanese, was shaped in this period probably more than in any other. But even though Yoshimasa played a leading part in the formation of Japanese taste, his achievements have not brought him a favorable reputation. Rather, he is most often depicted by historians as a spiritual weakling, completely under the dominance of his wife, Hino Tomiko. His extravagance, his incompetence in dealing with state business, and his inability to succor the people in times of famine or to end the meaningless Ōnin War are deplored, quite properly. And in the eyes of most historians, his virtues, particularly his encouragement of the arts, have not compensated for his faults.

Unfortunately, the surviving documents do not enable us to create a rounded portrait of Yoshimasa. We know many facts about his life, and they do help us visualize what it was like for him and others to live in the Japan of the fifteenth century, but neither his poems nor the facts of his private life enable us to come close to him. We can, however, imagine the salient features of his personality from his aesthetic preferences, especially after he had freed himself from shogunal duties and lived as he pleased at the Higashiyama retreat. We can tell, for example, that although he profoundly respected Yoshimitsu, he had no desire to emulate his grandfather's grandeur.

Perhaps Yoshimasa's preferences toward the end of his life were influenced to some extent by economic necessity: simple structures like those at the Higashiyama retreat cost less than an elaborately decorated palace. But surely that was not the main reason why the architecture at Higashiyama so little resembles that of the Kinkaku-ji, the Temple of the Golden Pavilion, built by Yoshimitsu. The simplicity and reliance on suggestion of the buildings and gardens at Higashiyama may indicate that a man who had earlier exhausted the pleasures of extravagance had at last achieved a kind of enlightenment. Yoshimasa's seeming incapability to act, even when warfare reached his doorstep, may also be interpreted not as the callous indifference of a tyrant but as the result of the despair felt by a civilized human being who could find no solution to endless warfare. It was less admirable, no doubt, to withdraw from the world than it would have been to face courageously the terrible problems facing Japan, but Yoshimasa's withdrawal from society enriched Japanese culture far more than any display of courage of which he might have been capable.

The retreat that Yoshimasa built in Higashiyama is popularly known as the Ginkaku-ji, or Temple of the Silver Pavilion, a name that appropriately suggests a humbler version of Yoshimitsu's Kinkaku-ji, or Temple of the Golden Pavilion, built some eighty years earlier. Unlike the gilded Kinkaku-ji, the Silver Pavilion was never decorated with silver leaf. The name instead suggests an age less brilliant than Yoshimitsu's Age of Gold. The arts that Yoshimasa favored—the tea ceremony, ink painting, the nō, and the rest—had the unobtrusive elegance of oxidized silver.

In 1449, the year when Yoshimasa assumed the duties of shogun, the reigning emperor was Go-Hanazono (1419–1470). Although he was shown respect, the emperor exercised little or no influence over the country's administration, and he hardly figures in histories of the period except as an accomplished *waka* poet. During the Ōnin War, when the palace where the emperor and former emperor lived was threatened by the fighting, both men moved without protest to Yoshimasa's palace at a word of command.

The emperor during the war, Go-Tsuchimikado (1442–1500; reigned from 1464), was not asked his preference between the two sides. He had no soldiers at his disposal and was protected only by the aura surrounding the throne. Unlike China, where dynasties were overthrown when they could no longer withstand their enemies, Japan had been ruled by a single dynasty from its earliest history, a fact that seems to have inhibited those (like Yoshimitsu) who could easily have seized the throne whenever they desired. The shogun ranked next in prestige after the emperor, though the old court ranks of chancellor (*kanpaku*) and the like still ranked higher in principle if not in fact.

In 1449 Japan was still largely controlled by the *bakufu*, the "tent government," or shogunate. The first shogun, Yoritomo (1147–1199), led soldiers of the Minamoto clan during its successful battles for power at the end of the twelfth century. Although the Minamoto were of noble lineage, Yoritomo had lived for most of his life away from the capital, and in 1192 when he established his *bakufu*, the first warrior government, he chose as the site Kamakura in the east, not far from modern Tokyo.

The *bakufu* was much better organized than earlier governments. It had well-organized administrative organs in Kamakura and maintained control over the rest of the country through estate stewards (*jitō*), whose loyalty in the wars had been rewarded with grants of the land they managed, and by constables (*shugo*), who were chosen from among vassals to maintain the peace in different parts of the country. Historians discuss the lord–vassal relationship prevailing under the Kamakura *bakufu* in terms of feudalism, even though the appropriateness of this European term has been questioned. The Kamakura *bakufu* ruled the country successfully for about 150 years. But the cost of the defeat of the two Mongol invasions in 1274 and 1281 put the Kamakura *bakufu* in serious economic difficulties, as victory over the Mongols had not brought the usual spoils of war (such as the lands of the defeated) that could be apportioned among meritorious vassals.

Civil war between the senior and junior lines descended from Emperor Go-Saga (1220–1272) also helped weaken the Kamakura *bakufu* at the end of the thirteenth century, and it finally was overthrown in 1333. Emperor Go-Daigo (1288–1339), who had been banished by the *bakufu* to the Oki Islands in the previous year for having planned a revolt against its authority, escaped and led the movement to restore executive power to the throne. His followers, at first few in number, won victories against *bakufu* troops, inducing other forces that had become discontent with the *bakufu* to join them. Chief of these allies was Ashikaga Takauji, a member of a branch of the Minamoto family that owned extensive estates. Takauji had been sent with a powerful army to defeat the supporters of Go-Daigo but then changed sides, ensuring victory for the imperial cause and the end of the Kamakura *bakufu*.

Go-Daigo, restored to the throne and possessing greater powers than any emperor had for many years, did not govern wisely. His decision to build a lavish new palace at a time when the treasury was exhausted resulted in unreasonable demands for funds from landowners and led to general discontent. The revival of direct imperial rule under Go-Daigo lasted for only three years.

Although he had been amply rewarded for his part in the revival of imperial power, Ashikaga Takauji became increasingly restive under the new regime. He was particularly angered by the haughty manners of the nobles surrounding Go-Daigo, who treated him as a boorish soldier. So he finally decided to change sides once again, this time with an eye to establishing a new *bakufu* with himself at the head.

A series of battles between Takauji and the forces loyal to Go-Daigo ended in 1336 with the emperor fleeing the capital, eventually taking refuge in the mountains of Yoshino. Takauji set up a prince of the northern line as the new emperor. Go-Daigo, refusing to abdicate, established a court in Yoshino, initiating a period of sixty years when there were two rival courts, one in Kyoto and the other in Yoshino. Takauji was appointed as shogun by the northern (Kyoto) emperor, and two years later, in 1338, he established his *bakufu* in Kyoto rather than in Kamakura. The Ashikaga *bakufu* lasted until 1588 when Yoshiaki, the fifteenth and last shogun, abdicated. Of the last seven shoguns, only Yoshimasa's son Yoshihisa (1465–1489) is more than a name in the Ashikaga family genealogy.

In retrospect, the Ashikaga period (also known as the Muromachi period after the section of Kyoto where Ashikaga Yoshimitsu built his "Palace of Flowers") might seem almost unrelievedly dark because of the wars and the way the wars affected the lives of members of the court and other educated people. If we turn, however, from those at the court to the humbler classes, as described in the popular fiction of the time,⁵ we find stories showing that despite the warfare, the period for many commoners was far from being a time of unvarying gloom. The hero of these stories is often a commoner who, by dint of hard work and mother wit, becomes fabulously rich and may even marry a princess. Granted that these stories are fiction and not fact, they could exert their appeal only if in some way they reflected the society. The Ashikaga period is frequently characterized as age of *gekokujō*, or those underneath conquering those above. The constant warfare, especially during the first half of the sixteenth century, caused meaningless slaughter and destroyed much of the heritage from the past, but it gave those of exceptional strength or intelligence a chance to rise above their station.

If *gekokujō* was welcome to those below, it was a nightmare to those above. Ichijō Kaneyoshi (1402–1481), the *kanpaku* at the time of the outbreak of the Ōnin War, was one of the most fortunate members of society. He enjoyed universal respect for his scholarship, had a large and distinguished family, and owned perhaps the finest library of the time. His house was destroyed in the fighting, but the library, because it was roofed with tiles and had earthen walls, withstood the fires that swept the city. "But," he recalled,

> bandits of the neighborhood, supposing that there must be money inside, soon broke their way in. They scattered the hundreds of boxes that had been the haunt of bookworms, and not one volume was left of all the Japanese and Chinese works that had been passed down in my family for over ten generations. I felt exactly like an old crane forced to leave its nest, or a blind man who has lost his stick.⁶

Even though he was the highest-ranking noble in the country, Kaneyoshi was forced to take refuge in Nara, where his son was the abbot of the great monastery Kōfuku-ji. He remained in exile from the capital for ten years.

While in Nara, Kaneyoshi devoted himself to a study of *The Tale of Genji* and other classics. The old culture, brutally mauled by the swords and flaming brands of ignorant soldiers, could still provide comfort and support to those like Kaneyoshi who looked back with longing to the Heian past. Others, not content with merely studying the classics, wrote pastiches in the language and manner of three hundred years earlier, only inadvertently betraying the fact that they lived in a totally dissimilar age.

Unlike the writers of the prose pastiches, the most important poets of the Higashiyama era wrote a new kind of poetry, *renga*, that had antecedents in traditional poetry but was distinctly of its own time. The other arts, whether visual or performing, were also essentially new and strongly influenced Japanese culture in the future. Under the guidance of the former shogun Ashikaga Yoshimasa, the Higashiyama era represented a kind of cultural renaissance in the wake of the worst destruction Japan had ever experienced.[7]

I

The assassination in 1441 of Ashikaga Yoshinori, the sixth shogun of the Ashikaga line, was carried out with exceptional efficiency and brutality. Assassinations of high-ranking persons were comparatively rare in Japan, at least until modern times, but a few are memorable: Sanetomo, the third Minamoto shogun, killed at the Tsurugaoka Shrine by his nephew, and Oda Nobunaga, murdered at the Honnō-ji by Akechi Mitsuhide. But about neither of these men was it said that he "died like a dog," as Gosukō-in (1372–1456) wrote of Yoshinori.[1]

Ashikaga Yoshinori (1394–1441), the third son of Yoshimitsu, had been sent (like many younger sons of high birth) to a Buddhist monastery for his education and preparation for a future career as a priest.

At an early age, thanks no doubt to family connections, he attained the exalted rank of *zasu* (abbot) of the Shōren-in, an important temple of the Tendai sect. His elder brother Yoshimochi (1386–1428), who had succeeded Yoshimitsu as shogun, abdicated in 1423 in favor of his son Yoshikazu (1407–1425). The young man, however, whose excessive indulgence in liquor and general dissolute conduct had earned him severe reprimands from his father, died of illness after only two years as shogun.

After resuming the post of shogun after Yoshikazu's death, Yoshimochi prayed for an heir at the Iwashimizu Hachiman Shrine, the ancestral shrine of the Minamoto clan (the clan to which the Ashikaga family belonged). He drew lots to see whether the god would accord this wish, and the desired answer was given: he would indeed have another son. Yoshimochi placed such great trust in the oracle that he felt it was unnecessary to designate a successor other than the unborn son. But his trust was misplaced: in 1428 Yoshimochi, who had not been favored with another son despite the oracle, developed a serious infection that seemed likely to prove fatal. The senior officials decided that they had no choice but to ask Yoshimochi directly for his choice of successor. The priest Mansai (1378–1435), who had served as "protecting priest" (*gojisō*) to the shogun, was delegated to go to the bedside of the dying Yoshimochi and ask him to designate his successor by name. Yoshimochi refused to name anyone. Mansai repeated the request several times, but still Yoshimochi refused, insisting that the successor be chosen by the senior retainers (*shūgi*).[2]

Mansai did finally succeed, however, in eliciting Yoshimochi's consent to draw lots to determine the successor. It was hoped that the god of the Hachiman Shrine, as guardian of the fortunes of the Ashikaga family, would choose a suitable man. Mansai wrote on slips of paper the names of four younger brothers of Yoshimochi. The slips, in elaborately sealed envelopes, were taken to the Iwashimizu Hachiman Shrine by the shogunal deputy (*kanrei*)

Hatakeyama Mitsuie (1372–1433) so that he might draw the lots in the presence of the god. The lot that Mitsuie drew, which was opened as soon as Yoshimochi died, bore the name of Gien, the abbot of the Shōren-in.[3]

Some scholars believe that the drawing of lots was rigged and that no matter which one had been drawn, it would have been inscribed with Gien's name. But as Imatani Akira convincingly argued, drawing lots was not a matter of mere chance to the people of that time: everyone involved was convinced that the choice was made by the god himself. In terms of such faith in the god's responsiveness to the Ashikaga family's prayers, it was unthinkable that anyone would have dared tamper with the slips.[4] At this distance from the events, we may wonder—even if we accept the genuineness of the drawing of lots—whether the god did not make a serious mistake in choosing Gien, the future Yoshinori, as the next shogun.

When it was discovered that Gien had won the lottery, he was informed that he would have to return to the laity. At first he expressed unwillingness to leave the priesthood, but eventually he convinced himself that his elevation to the rank of shogun had been the wish of the god and that he was therefore obliged to obey. His belief in the efficacy of drawing lots as a manner of discovering the will of the gods was further illustrated four months after he succeeded as shogun, when he proposed that a land dispute be settled by lots. In later years, other important decisions, ranging from the selection of the editor of an imperially sponsored anthology of poetry to the appointment of a priest for the Inner Shrine at Ise, were made according to lots drawn at Shinto shrines.

During his reign as shogun, Yoshinori displayed an undoubted executive capability, maintaining order in a country that was divided into "principalities," some of which rivaled the shogunate in military and economic strength. He also was a man of considerable culture who could take part in a *renga* session without disgracing himself. He stands out, however, not for his capability as shogun or for his cultural attainments but for the ferocity of his temper. In 1434 the nobleman Nakayama Sadachika (1401–1459) recorded in his diary that up to this date eighty high-ranking persons had been disposed of by Yoshinori's order, including fifty-nine members of the nobility, headed by a former *kanpaku*.[5]

Many were harshly punished for trivial offenses. One noble incurred Yoshinori's wrath merely because he smiled while serving as a torchbearer at a ceremony. On another occasion (in 1433) when the crowd watching a cockfight near Ichijō Kaneyoshi's residence got in the way of the shogun's procession, the enraged Yoshinori not only prohibited further cockfights at the Ichijō mansion but ordered that all chickens be driven from the capital.[6] Again, when a retainer offered the shogun a splendid plum tree, Yoshinori was angered to discover that one of the middle branches had been broken. The three gardeners who had transported the tree were imprisoned for breaking the branch, and an order was issued for the arrest of five retainers of the man who had presented the tree. Three of these men fled for their lives, and the other two committed suicide. In 1435 when Yoshinori traveled to Ise, he was annoyed by the tastelessness of the food he was served. The cook, albeit a samurai, was unceremoniously sent back to Kyoto. After Yoshinori had returned to the capital, the cook, all fear and trembling, again appeared in his presence. He was immediately arrested and beheaded. Two years later, three other cooks were executed for the same crime.[7]

These people do not rank among the important victims murdered by command of Yoshinori. Rather, he tended to find grounds for suspecting even high-ranking daimyos of harboring treacherous intentions, and when he thought they might be dangerous, he did not hesitate to provoke them into committing an offense. In the seventh month of 1431, a ceremony was held at which Yoshinori, following an old custom, ranked his generals in order of merit. Isshiki Yoshitsura (1400–1440) was named second best. He was offended because his grandfather had been ranked first by Ashikaga Yoshimitsu, and he thought he deserved the same distinction. Pleading illness, he declined to take part in the ceremony. This, predictably, infuriated Yoshinori, whose first impulse was to confiscate all of Yoshitsura's lands. Although he was dissuaded from taking such drastic action, he never forgave him, and when he judged the moment for revenge had come, he ordered Yoshitsura's death.[8]

Yoshinori's reign of terror was small in scale when compared with similar periods of imperial persecution in China, but in Japan there was no precedent for the bloodthirsty cruelty Yoshinori showed toward those who displeased him. During the Heian period, not one person in high office was executed for his crimes,[9] the worst punishment being banishment. Even during later periods, when a shogunate ruled the country, there was a reluctance to resort to capital punishment. Instead, serious offenses were usually punished by confiscation of property or (in the case of nobles) by loss of the privilege of attending court. Partly because it contrasted so greatly with the policies of earlier times, Yoshinori's persecution inspired dread, especially among nobles and daimyos who feared that they might be suspected of being disloyal. This fear led to sycophancy among those who surrounded Yoshinori, each man desperately eager to assure him of complete submission to his will. Wherever Yoshinori went, he could be sure of receiving costly gifts from men of the locality who craved to demonstrate their loyalty. No one dared to remonstrate with the shogun in the manner prescribed in Confucian texts for those who advised men in power.

Yoshinori was not easily convinced of the loyalty of those around him. In order to feel absolutely secure, he reversed the tendency toward rule by consensus that had evolved and instead most often acted like a bloodthirsty tyrant. His first response to any act that seemed to be disloyal was an order to kill. When the heads of his enemies were sent to the capital, he personally inspected them, to satisfy himself that the heads were not those of imposters. After the fall of Yūki Castle, the stronghold of one of Yoshinori's chief enemies, some fifty heads were sent to Kyoto for his inspection. Although they had been pickled in saké, in the intense heat of the Kyoto summer their features had decomposed and lost all semblance of their original appearance. The nobles had little desire to participate in the head inspection or even to get a glimpse of the unspeakably horrible sight, but they hurried to the spot, buckling on borrowed swords, each trying to be among the first to offer congratulations and fearful of incurring the shogun's wrath if he arrived late.

Any account of Yoshinori's actions is likely to make him seem so devoid of human feelings that one wonders how it was possible for a man whose early life had been spent in a monastery to forget so completely the Buddhist proscription on taking life. But he had not quite forgotten religion. After a major victory over pretenders to the position of shogun, when he at last decided that not one enemy of his regime was left on earth, he not only took part in the elaborate celebrations of victory staged by his sycophants but made pious pilgrimages to Buddhist temples and Shinto shrines to express thanks for the victory bestowed.

In the sixth month of 1441, Yoshinori received an invitation from members of the Akamatsu family to visit their house to celebrate his triumph over the Yūki family and particularly his success in tracking down and putting to death two boys of twelve and ten years who might have been used to restore the Yūki fortunes. The Akamatsu family had a tradition, dating back to Ashikaga Yoshimitsu's childhood, of staging *matsubayashi*—festive dances performed early in the New Year in honor of the shogun. The tradition had lapsed after Yoshimitsu expressed a preference for *sarugaku* (nō) in celebrating the New Year, but it was revived in 1429, and since then *matsubayashi* had been performed every year at the shogun's palace. For the New Year of 1441, however, there was no performance of *matsubayashi*. It was announced that the head of the family, Akamatsu Mitsusuke (1373–1441), would be unable to attend the shogun's court because he had lost his senses. His younger brother, Mochisada, had not long before run afoul of Yoshinori when an affair with a lady-in-waiting was brought to light and his estates were confiscated. Rumor had it that Mitsusuke would be next to experience the shogun's wrath. Acting like a madman was probably the best way of deflecting Yoshinori's suspicions. The strategy worked for a time, but there was no way of telling what might next provoke Yoshinori's rage.

The invitation to Yoshinori mentioned that this year there was an unusually large number of ducks in the garden pond. The shogun, it predicted, would surely enjoy watching parent and baby ducks cavorting in the water. Accustomed to dining out almost every night at the houses of his officials, Yoshinori accepted the invitation and arrived at the Akamatsu residence on the afternoon of the twenty-fourth day of the sixth month, accompanied by a retinue of nine provincial governors (*shugo*) and other high officials, almost all of whom owed their position to Yoshinori. The host this day was Akamatsu Noriyasu, Mitsusuke's heir. Mitsusuke himself, because of his alleged madness, did not appear.

After admiring the ducks and ducklings on the pond, the shogun and his party were offered drinks and other refreshments. The entertainment was lavish, with a full program of nō to be offered for the shogun's diversion. It was gradually growing dark as the third nō play was performed. Another round of drinks was passed around, and the guests were in a genial mood. Suddenly a thumping, as of drums, could be heard from somewhere in back of the house. The tipsy shogun opened his eyes and demanded what had caused the noise. A senior official replied nonchalantly that it might be thunder. The thumping, it later turned out, was caused when horses tied up in the stable were released by Mitsusuke's grooms and set running in the garden. Voices called out, "Shut the gates!" and servants bolted the outer gates, ostensibly to keep the horses from running away but actually to prevent anyone from leaving the house.

Soon afterward, several dozen armed men burst in from an adjacent room. Two men, grasping Yoshinori from either side, pinned him down onto the tatami. He cried out, "Wait!" only for a third man, Azumi Yukihide, to lop off his head. Four of the daimyos in Yoshinori's party, in a state of panic, managed to make an ignominious escape by crawling from the room and climbing over the garden wall; they saved their necks at the cost of becoming laughingstocks of the town. A few, more courageous than the rest, unsheathed their swords and charged against the Akamatsu men. Most were killed on the spot or died later of their wounds. Madenokōji Tokifusa (1394–1457) wrote in his diary that this was an unspeakable event without precedent in all of history, an opinion shared by other nobles who kept diaries.[10] Akamatsu Mitsusuke, who was supposed to be hopelessly insane, showed himself at this point and made plain that he had been the leader of the plot to kill the shogun. The Akamatsu retainers, after first setting fire to their residence, successfully made their escape. Azumi Yukihide, the man who had cut off Yoshinori's head, took it with him, held high on a pike. Mitsusuke, it was reported, looked greatly pleased, as if he had realized a long-cherished desire. Nobody attempted to pursue the Akamatsu retainers that day.

Seeing flames rise over the Akamatsu house, Tokifusa rushed to the palace to inform Emperor Go-Hanazono. The blinds had been drawn at dusk, but the emperor went outside to look at the flames in the distance. As yet nobody knew what had happened, but gradually the names of wounded survivors reached the palace. Yoshinori was not among them, and it was feared that he had been killed. Finally, a report arrived from Hosokawa Mochiyuki (1400–1442), the *kanrei*, telling in detail of the terrible event. But he reassured the court that there would be no break in the succession, that Yoshinori's young son would be the next shogun. He appealed to the entire population to remain calm.

That night, monks from the Shōkoku-ji, a temple intimately associated with the Ashikaga family, came to search for Yoshinori's headless body in the ruins of the Akamatsu mansion. They eventually found the blackened corpse, placed it in a coffin they had brought with them, and carried it to Rokuon-in, a subtemple of the Shōkoku-ji. The next day, the coffin was taken to the Tōji-in, another subtemple, for interment. The funeral service was not held for another two weeks.

That day the various daimyos met at the *bakufu* headquarters to discuss what to do in such an unprecedented situation. They agreed that Yoshinori's oldest son, Yoshikatsu, then known as Sen'yachamaru, was the only possible successor. The boy, barely seven years old, was obviously incapable of performing as shogun, so the daimyos decided to revive the Council of Elders and to entrust it with selecting governmental policies, thereby reverting to the practice before 1435 when Yoshinori first wielded unrestricted power. Hosokawa Mochiyuki remained the shogunal deputy, but his cowardly behavior at the time of the assassination had cost him the esteem of the other daimyos.

At this time, a messenger from the Akamatsu family came to Mochiyuki's house saying that Yoshinori's head was at Nakajima in Settsu Province and that Mitsusuke intended to hold a service for the head. Afraid that the visit from an Akamatsu retainer might be interpreted as a sign of collusion between the Akamatsu family and himself, Mochiyuki gave orders for the messenger to be beheaded. When Mitsusuke learned that his messenger had been executed, he left for his fief in Harima to the west of Settsu, taking Yoshinori's head with him. He also called off the planned religious service.

Kakitsu monogatari, a romanticized account of events at this time, states that once he had reached his stronghold in Harima on the twenty-fourth day of the sixth month, Mitsusuke conducted a ceremony of cremation of Yoshinori's head at the Ankoku-ji.[11] Dressed in a white *hitatare*—a formal outer robe, worn chiefly by high-ranked military men—Mitsusuke went before a raised platform covered with brocade of golden ground. Placing the head on the brocade, he bowed respectfully and then painstakingly described to the head the great services his family had rendered to the Ashikaga clan. His address opened in this manner:

> The Akamatsu family for generations has striven for the good of the realm. It has suppressed rebellious elements and, never wavering in its loyalty, has proved its capability at performing its duties. For this reason, when the shogun Takauji, who had been defeated in battle in the capital and forced to flee, asked the help of the Akamatsu family, the family, with troops from our three fiefs, built the castle of Shirahata in Kinoyama and for three years successfully defended it against armies from many parts of the country. This castle, which had no equal in the realm, to the end was never taken.[12]

Mitsusuke related many other instances of Akamatsu loyalty to the shoguns, even when fighting against seemingly hopeless odds; but, he declared, Yoshinori had forgotten the many deeds that bespoke the clan's extraordinary loyalty and had plotted instead to destroy it. An ancestor of Yoshinori (probably a reference to Takauji) had seven times sworn an oath to Hachiman that if the Akamatsu perished, the Ashikaga would also perish. The present incident (the assassination) had occurred because Yoshinori had forgotten his ancestor's oath. Mitsusuke never had anticipated that such events would occur, but now he was sure that pursuers would soon come after him from Kyoto to avenge the shogun's death. When that happened, he would commit *seppuku* and, in the spirit of the oath sworn by Takauji, would accompany Ashikaga Yoshinori to the afterworld. If by chance his life should last a bit longer, he would devote every hour to heartfelt prayers for Yoshinori's salvation. So saying, he took the head, which was wrapped in a cloak, and, turning it up to face him, three times did it reverence. All present, carried away by the scene, wetted the sleeves of their *hitatare* with their tears. The head was placed in a sandalwood cart and carried to the spot where it was cremated. This, the *Kakitsu monogatari* informs us, was an instance of requiting hatred with kindness.[13]

This account, obviously the work of a partisan of Mitsusuke, is consciously literary, almost comically so in its mention of soldiers weeping so copiously that they had to wring the tears from their sleeves, but perhaps it contains an element of truth. Modern historians usually interpret the assassination in terms of Mitsusuke's fear that Yoshinori intended to bestow his three fiefs on a rival in the Akamatsu family, but Mitsusuke may have been angered not only by the threat to his lands but also by the ingratitude Yoshinori had displayed to a family that had served the Ashikaga family well. Or perhaps Mitsusuke's tender concern for the head was inspired by fear that Yoshinori's wrathful spirit might come back to haunt the Akamatsu family.

Yoshikatsu could not immediately be proclaimed as shogun because, not having had his *genbuku* (coming-of-age) ceremony, he was officially still a child. (He had the ceremony in the following year at the extraordinarily early age of eight and then was named the shogun.) Nevertheless, Yoshikatsu was the highest-ranking member of the shogunate. It must have been unsettling for senior constables and other military officers to bow before a small boy by way of manifesting their loyalty, but probably they recognized that somebody—even a child—was needed at the apex of the *bakufu*.

After succeeding to his father's office, Yoshikatsu moved to the Muromachi Palace along with six younger brothers. All were potential candidates for the office of shogun if Yoshikatsu should die. In addition, there were some surviving sons of Ashikaga

Yoshimitsu, now serving as high-ranking priests at various temples, who might succeed. Fearing that Akamatsu Mitsusuke might try to set up one of these priests as shogun in place of Yoshikatsu, Hosokawa Mochiyuki had all three kept under house arrest.

On the sixth day of the seventh month, a public funeral was held for Yoshinori at the Tōji-in. Kikei Shinzui (1401–1469), the chief priest of the Rokuon-in, feeling responsible as a member of the Akamatsu family for the loss of Yoshinori's head, had decided some days earlier to go to Harima, at the risk of his life, to obtain the head for the funeral. Shinzui succeeded in having an audience with Mitsusuke, who was impressed by his sincerity. Because Hosokawa Mochiyuki had twice earlier beheaded messengers sent by Mitsusuke, it would not have been surprising if Mitsusuke had meted out the same punishment to an envoy sent by his enemies, but he willingly surrendered Yoshinori's head. If the account in *Kakitsu monogatari* is to be believed, the head had already been cremated, but it would not have been difficult to substitute another: given the heat of the summer, the real or false head of Yoshinori would probably have become unrecognizable in a few weeks. Even if the head that Mitsusuke surrendered was genuine, he had already enjoyed to the full his vengeance over Yoshinori and no longer needed the head as a reminder of his triumph. His thoughts were undoubtedly on the coming battle with the forces of the shogunate.

Mitsusuke expected that a major shogunate army would come pursuing him at almost any moment, and once he was in Harima, he took appropriate measures to defend himself. The punitive army, however, was strangely slow in leaving Kyoto. Mitsusuke apparently got tired of waiting, and on the eighth day of the seventh month he sent a letter to the shogunal deputy Hosokawa Mochiuji challenging him to send an army after him.[14] When this failed to produce any result, it occurred to Mitsusuke that he might set up a member of the Ashikaga family as a rival to Yoshikatsu. He found a suitable man, a Zen priest whom he persuaded to return to the laity under the name of Yoshitaka. It was in Yoshitaka's name that Mitsusuke issued a message to samurai in all parts of the country asking them to stand behind him. Mitsusuke, the murderer of the shogun, was now also a traitor.[15]

On the twenty-fifth day of the sixth month, a decision was reached at a meeting of the *bakufu* to put down the Akamatsu revolt, but implementation of the decision was repeatedly delayed. Yamana Mochitoyo (Sōzen, 1404–1473),[16] the commander of the punitive force, at first showed no inclination to leave for the front, saying it was premature. Even the few units that were actually dispatched to Harima did little more than reconnoiter the terrain at the border. In the meantime, a series of small incidents estranged Sōzen from the shogunal deputy Hosokawa Mochiyuki, who reportedly had urged his troops to destroy the Yamana family before attacking the Akamatsu. But there was no semblance of unity in the punitive army, and its cause was unpopular: far from being considered an enemy of the people, Akamatsu Mitsusuke was acclaimed in Kyoto for having delivered them from an evil shogun.

The *bakufu* army finally left Kyoto on the eleventh day of the seventh month, but the leadership was still far from unified. The shogunal deputy, worried about the situation, decided to ask the emperor for an edict calling for the punishment of the Akamatsu family for its crime in assassinating the shogun. Although the emperor had no troops with which to reinforce the punitive army, his blessing would strengthen and unify the disparate forces, just as the brocade pennant carried by the imperial forces in the battle fought in 1868 between troops loyal to the emperor and those of the shogun proved of critical importance in the defeat of the shogun's army.

Mochiyuki sent for Madenokōji Tokifusa and explained why he needed imperial authorization: "People are surely aware that because the shogun is a minor, it is up to the shogunal deputy to issue orders, but I feel so uneasy about this that I would like to request an imperial edict."[17] Tokifusa was dubious about the appropriateness of issuing such an edict, which in the past (and even then very seldom) had been used only when asking that enemies of the court be punished, but Mochiyuki desperately needed the edict to bolster his forces. The emperor's sanction carried the weight of the ultimate source of authority.

On the thirtieth day of the seventh month, Emperor Go-Hanazono decided to grant Mochiyuki's request for an imperial edict. Tokifusa was commanded to compose the edict immediately. He asked for a day's respite, pointing out that it was an unlucky day in the calendar, but he was refused, and he was obliged to set about writing the edict without delay. When the first version was completed, it was sent to a Confucian scholar for stylistic corrections. The rough draft was then sent to the emperor for his approval. He made extensive corrections, mainly of a moralistic nature, but the meaning was generally the same as in Tokifusa's text:

> The conspiracy of Akamatsu Mitsusuke and his son Noriyasu has disturbed public law and order; they have blocked the imperial rule in Harima and brought on war with those who obey the will of Heaven. For this reason, no time should be lost in dispatching an army to chastise these enemies. Now is the moment for each man to display complete loyalty to the country and filial piety to his family. Do not allow further days to pass without action. As for those who have cooperated with the conspirators, they should definitely be punished for the same crime. This is Our command.[18]

Although Akamatsu Mitsusuke had three domains—Bizen and Mimasaka as well as Harima—he decided to concentrate his forces in Harima. The advancing *bakufu* army quickly took Mimasaka, but by the end of the seventh month the two armies were locked in a stalemate. In the middle of the eighth month, Hosokawa Mochiyuki persuaded the military governor of Awaji to attack the

Akamatsu positions from the sea. The simultaneous attack from land and sea came as an unexpected surprise to the Akamatsu army and led to a forced retreat. The shogunate troops, led by Yamana Sōzen, broke into Harima on the twenty-eighth day of the eighth month, and on the thirtieth a hard-fought engagement between the two armies ended with the defeat of the Akamatsu force. On the third of the ninth month, Sakamoto Castle, the stronghold of the Akamatsu family, fell to Sōzen.

With a handful of his retainers, Mitsusuke managed to escape to Kinoyama. Aided by local samurai, they made a last stand at Kinoyama Castle. The final attack began at dawn on the tenth day of the ninth month. By nine in the morning, it was clear that the Yamana troops would soon take the castle keep. Mitsusuke summoned his son Noriyasu and his younger brother Norishige and ordered them to escape so that they might continue warfare against the *bakufu*. Both men had been deeply involved in the assassination and subsequent events and wanted to commit *seppuku* along with Mitsusuke, but they could not disregard his last wish.

Once Mitsusuke had watched the two men safely escape, he committed *seppuku*, after commanding Azumi Yukihide to serve as his second and cut off his head. Mitsusuke's suicide was followed by those of some fifty of his retainers. Azumi, who had cut off the head of the shogun two and a half months earlier, set fire to the keep and leaped into the flames.

2

It took two and a half months for the shogunate
to avenge the death of the shogun. The victory over
Akamatsu Mitsusuke was won entirely by troops
under the command of the Yamana family, because
the forces of other daimyos loyal to the shogunate
arrived too late to participate in the final assault.[1]
Mitsusuke's head, retrieved from the blackened
ruins of Kinoyama Castle, was sent to the capital as
proof of the victory, but Yamana Sōzen, the chief of
the Yamana army, decided not to return to Kyoto for
the pleasure of a triumphal return. Instead, his
forces, in the name of ending resistance from surviving Akamatsu adherents and obtaining remunera-
tion for the cost of the war, plundered Harima
Province.

Sōzen's decision not to return to Kyoto may have been influenced by word he had received of an outbreak of peasant uprisings (*tsuchi ikki*) in the capital and the neighboring region. Late in the eighth month of 1441, peasants were threatening Kyoto from several sides. Arrows had already been traded between the peasants and the soldiers of Kyōgoku Mochikiyo (1407–1470), the military governor of Ōmi, the domain where the uprising had originated. The peasants were demanding an "act of grace" (*tokusei*) to cancel their debts. This was not the first time peasants (and other malcontents) had banded together for the purpose of obtaining a *tokusei*, but the uprising was on a larger scale and better organized than any previous confrontation between peasants and shogunate troops had been. Bands of armed peasants, generally a thousand or so men each, were stationed at the strategic accesses to the capital. They were led by local samurai (*jizamurai*) who chose to identify themselves with the peasants of the domains where they lived rather than with the feudal lords they served.

The initial targets of the peasants were saké breweries and storehouses. The owners were not only the most conspicuous possessors of wealth but also the chief moneylenders. Temples that practiced moneylending (though they disguised their profits as "gifts" from parishioners for temple repairs) were also subjected to the wrath of the peasants, who assaulted storehouses and temples alike, seizing debt documents and burning them.

The shogunate lacked sufficient strength to suppress the uprisings. The bulk of its troops were off in Harima in pursuit of Akamatsu Mitsusuke, leaving only skeleton forces under Kyōgoku Mochikiyo's command to protect the capital, and the best these troops could do was maintain a hold on the gateway to eastern Japan at Awata, leaving all the other gateways to the city at the mercy of the rebels. It surely was no accident that the uprising occurred in the wake of the confusion caused by the murder of the shogun.[2]

Even before fighting broke out in the capital, a *tokusei* had been issued by the intendants of two manors in Ōmi Province.[3] It provided that all debts, mortgages, and mutual financing plans (*tanomoshikō*) be annulled and that pawned objects be redeemed by payment of one-eleventh of the amount due. Although this *tokusei* applied to only a particular region of Ōmi, probably others of similar content were issued elsewhere at about the same time.

Proclamations of *tokusei* became common as the weakened shogunate desperately sought to buy time by making concessions to rebellious peasants. The threat of an impending *tokusei* naturally caused prospective moneylenders to be very cautious about parting with their money, and contracts with borrowers often included the proviso that the money had to be returned even if a *tokusei* were issued.

Pressure mounted from peasant uprisings as it became clear that the shogunate troops lacked sufficient strength to protect the capital. The area of the imperial palace and the shogunate's headquarters was particularly vulnerable. Although the shogunate managed with difficulty to hold off this threat, peasant soldiers were able to overrun the southern part of the city, including the great temple Tōji. They threatened the priests, declaring that if they failed to get a *tokusei* from the shogun, they would set the temple afire. No doubt they hoped that the shogunate would yield rather than allow a major Buddhist temple to be destroyed. They probably hoped also that the Tōji monks would exert pressure to preserve the temple from danger.

The new shogun, Ashikaga Yoshikatsu, a boy of seven, could not be expected to organize defenses that might prevent peasant rebels from invading the capital. The shogunal deputy, Hosokawa Mochiyuki, also refrained from taking action, probably because he was waiting for the army to return from Harima. In the meantime, peasants surrounded the city, and some detachments even entered the city itself, indiscriminately setting fire to buildings.[4] Following the example of those who had occupied the Tōji, other bands captured temples and threatened to burn them down unless the shogunate granted a *tokusei*. It was ironic that these men were using brute force to obtain a *tokusei*, a term that literally means "virtuous rule."

With each day that passed, the situation in the city grew more desperate. The minister of the center, Saionji Kinna (1411–1468), wrote in *Kankenki*, his diary, on the seventh day of the ninth month: "The peasant uprising began out of a demand for a *tokusei*. Now they have blocked the seven gateways into the capital. There is nothing on sale anymore, and the capital is doomed to starve. An unspeakable state of affairs."[5]

People in the city gradually became aware that the shogunate had no plan whatsoever for suppressing the rebellion. Deciding they had no choice but to defend their property themselves, storehouse owners hired ruffians (including criminals) as guards. At times there were violent clashes between the guards and the peasants that usually ended with storehouses burning down. But despite the unsettled conditions prevailing in the city, the Chrysanthemum Festival was celebrated with customary rites in the imperial palace on the ninth day of the ninth month, the court maintaining its studied aloofness from the surrounding warfare.

Word reached Kyoto on the twelfth of the ninth month that Kinoyama Castle, the last stronghold of Akamatsu's supporters, had fallen. The news served to increase the activity of the peasants besieging Kyoto, who feared that the victory might result in the return of large numbers of shogunate troops to Kyoto, thereby ending their own control of the approaches to the city. Demands for a *tokusei* grew more strident as the conviction spread that the peasants' siege of Kyoto would be successful now or never. The shogunate finally bowed to the pressure and agreed to issue a *tokusei* canceling commoners' debts. But the peasants insisted that this relief be extended to the whole of society, including the nobles and the samurai, and threatened to resume fighting if this demand were refused. Madenokōji Tokifusa interpreted this seemingly disinterested gesture of concern for the nobility to the peasants' fear of reprisals once the shogunate had recouped its strength; that is, including nobles and samurai in the *tokusei* would probably make them more sympathetic to the peasants' cause.

The long-awaited *tokusei* was finally issued on the fourteenth day of the ninth month. This was the first time in the history of Japan that the government had bowed in this manner to demands of the common people. The decree, promulgated in the name of Kyōgoku Mochikiyo, was pasted on the walls of the Council of Retainers (Samuraidokoro) and displayed at prominent places inside the city and at the seven gateways. It applied to everyone, regardless of class.

Madenokōji Tokifusa was rescued by the *tokusei* from a heavy accumulation of debts, but he could not help but feel ashamed to be the beneficiary of a dispensation that had been extorted from the shogunate by a lawless peasantry. At first he refused to take advantage of the *tokusei* to free himself of debts, but he changed his mind when he heard the rumor that in order to protect themselves from possible future *tokusei*, pawnbrokers were going to raise interest rates and confiscate all pawned articles not redeemed within three months. Tokifusa decided therefore to comply with the *tokusei* and redeem at bargain prices the articles he had pawned, privately promising himself to compensate the pawnbroker at some future date. He did not forget that he was a member of the nobility, and the promise was his way of preserving his dignity, though (no less than the peasants) he was desperately eager to be free of debt.

As soon as the edict was issued, members of the peasant uprising stormed into the storehouses, concealing their faces behind masks so as to forestall possible future incrimination. The moneylenders, helpless in the face of the decree, had no choice but to turn over pledges of repayment. The peasants, somewhat mollified, opened two of the gateways to the capital, allowing food to enter, but the other five remained blockaded. Food and other necessities were in gravely short supply.

On the seventeenth of the ninth month, the heads of Akamatsu Mitsusuke and those of his followers who had committed suicide reached Kyoto. They were inspected first by the shogunal deputy Hosokawa Mochiyuki, who was familiar enough with the features of these men to identify the heads, even though they had been charred by the fire. The heads were next taken to the shogun, Yoshikatsu (still known by his childhood name Sen'yachamaru), the designated successor of Ashikaga Yoshinori, for his inspection. The boy probably had never before seen Akamatsu Mitsusuke or the others, and even if he had, he could scarcely be expected to identify their blackened heads, but the head inspection ceremony was carried out with due solemnity by way of confirming his authority as the future shogun. It is not difficult to imagine the traumatic effect that the sight of the heads probably produced on little Sen'yachamaru.

The heads of Akamatsu Mitsusuke and Azumi Yukihide (the man who had beheaded Yoshinori) were paraded through the streets of Kyoto on the twenty-first of the ninth month. The feelings of those who watched as the heads passed by were probably mixed. The executed men, denounced as traitors to the shogunate, had been punished accordingly; but it was hard to forget that it was thanks to their crime that Yoshinori's age of terror had been brought to an end. After the heads had been carried through the streets, they were nailed to the prison gate.

The blockade of the city was gradually lifted, but the peasants were still entrenched in temple buildings, and the uprising did not end until well into the next month.[6] For the next twenty years, peace was generally maintained throughout the country, largely by the issuance of *tokusei*. The pattern of peasant unrest leading to a *tokusei*, established in 1441, was frequently repeated, not only during the remainder of the Muromachi period but until the end of the age of civil warfare in the sixteenth century.

Two events—the assassination of the shogun and the issuance of the first *tokusei*, both in 1441—marked a turning point in the history of the Muromachi shogunate. Yoshinori had been a blood-thirsty dictator, but he had also been a commanding figure who controlled the warlords by force of his personality, if not by actual military strength. Some scholars believe that Yoshinori's reign marked the high point of the shogunate's effective administration of the country. None of Yoshinori's successors possessed his innate ability to command. His death also brought to the fore the enmity between the Yamana and Hosokawa clans that precipitated the Ōnin War twenty-five years later.

As the result of his success in tracking down and killing Mitsusuke, Yamana Sōzen acquired three important provinces that had been in the possession of the Akamatsu family. The Akamatsu were not, however, exterminated, and remnants of this once powerful family rose again with the encouragement of the Hosokawa, who revealed themselves in an increasingly open manner as enemies of the Yamana.

The strongest figure in the shogunate after Yoshinori's death was the shogunal deputy Hosokawa Mochiyuki, who took over the government and arranged for the recognition of Yoshikatsu as the next shogun. The fact that Yoshikatsu's mother was Hino Shigeko (1411–1463) may initially have been an obstacle to his succession. Although Shigeko had been Yoshinori's consort, he dismissed her from this position after losing his temper over what he deemed to be the insolent behavior of her brother, Hino Yoshisuke. Yoshinori replaced Shigeko with a concubine named Ōgimachisanjō Tadako. Yoshisuke was put under house arrest, and Yoshinori refused to listen to pleas that he be forgiven. Instead, one summer night he sent men to murder Yoshisuke as he slept under mosquito netting. Yoshisuke's property was confiscated and turned over to one of Yoshinori's subordinates.

The entire Hino family was now in disgrace. Ever since Yoshimitsu's time, all the shoguns' consorts had been Hino women, much as the consorts of Heian-period emperors had almost always been chosen from the Fujiwara family. Yoshinori's new consort, however, came from a distinguished noble family that was on bad terms with the Hino.

Despite his extreme youth and his mother's unfortunate family connections, Yoshikatsu succeeded his father as shogun, partly because the precaution had been taken of persuading Ōgimachisanjō Tadako to adopt him as her son, but mainly because of Hosokawa Mochiyuki's political skill. He not only secured the agreement of the other major daimyos to Yoshikatsu's succession but also acted as a conscientious adviser to the boy shogun. Yoshikatsu began his studies in the second month of 1442. In the eleventh month, on the same day of his *genbuku* ceremony, he was given the court title of Middle General of the Left Palace Guards and proclaimed as shogun.

The peasant uprising was the most notable event of the new shogun's brief reign. As long as Mochiyuki was guiding Yoshikatsu, it seemed likely that the boy would develop into a capable shogun, but Mochiyuki died in 1442, and the office of shogunal deputy passed to Hatakeyama Mochikuni (1397–1455). Unlike his predecessor, Mochikuni had no interest in guiding Yoshikatsu or restoring the authority of the shogunate; instead, he was absorbed in waging a private war with the Hosokawa for supremacy.[7] His machinations were foiled when a dispute divided the Hatakeyama family into two factions, one supporting Mochikuni's illegitimate son and the other favoring his adopted son as the next head of the family.

The alliances and disputes of the warrior families at this time are hard to remember because the sides changed so often and the names of the participants were so similar. (Mochitoyo, Mochikuni, and Mochiyuki were the personal names of important men belonging to three rival families.) It may be more rewarding to consider why one or another of the major military governors did not

attempt to seize the office of shogun. The shogunate was particularly weak at this time. When Ashikaga Yoshimasa became shogun,
it controlled only Shikoku and the central part and provinces at the
western end of Honshū. The Kantō region and Kyūshū, in the
hands of local rulers, paid no attention to the shogunate's orders.
In addition to the shogunate's fundamental weakness, there was the
particular problem of its being headed by a boy shogun. Neither
Yoshikatsu nor his successor, his younger brother Yoshimasa,
inspired men to fight in their behalf. For all their bowing before
the shogun and their oaths of fidelity, the military governors did
not take seriously a child of seven or eight as their commanding
general. They may, however, have found it convenient to have a
figurehead shogun who could easily be manipulated and did not
belong to any faction. They may also have had lingering feelings of
loyalty to the Ashikaga family, rather like their respect for the
imperial house, that made even the most powerful military governor hesitate to attempt to usurp the office of shogun.

Yoshikatsu died of dysentery in 1443, leaving the office of
shogun vacant once again.[8] His younger brother Yoshimasa[9] succeeded him, but the choice was by no means automatic. Yoshinori
had other sons, any one of whom might have been chosen. The
decision in Yoshimasa's favor was made by the shogunal deputy
Hatakeyama Mochikuni. Even though Yoshikatsu's succession had
been hampered by the unpopularity of his mother, Hino Shigeko,
Mochikuni apparently chose Yoshimasa precisely because his
mother was the same Shigeko. Popular or not, she was still a figure
to be reckoned with.[10]

Two months after Yoshimasa was installed as head of the Ashikaga family in 1443, some thirty or forty self-styled adherents of
the Southern Court[11] broke into the imperial palace and stole two
of three imperial regalia—the sword and the sacred jewels—and
carried them off to the Enryaku-ji, the Tendai monastery on
Mount Hiei. Three days later, a government force commanded by

Mochikuni climbed Mount Hiei and returned with the heads of the chief conspirators but without the regalia. The sword was recovered elsewhere, but the jewels remained in the hands of Southern Court adherents for another ten years. The incident made a dismal beginning for Yoshimasa's reign.[12]

The attack on the palace and the loss of the regalia naturally caused great alarm, and there were disquieting rumors that the Hosokawa, the Yamana, and other daimyos were secretly opposed to Yoshimasa. As the shogunal deputy, Hatakeyama Mochikuni had the authority to put down resistance to his choice of shogun, but the Hosokawa family showed increasing hostility to Mochikuni and in 1445 succeeded in replacing him as shogunal deputy with Hosokawa Katsumoto (1430–1473), a son of Hosokawa Mochiyuki. Katsumoto was only fifteen years old at the time, but his marriage to a daughter of Yamana Sōzen enhanced his standing. Although the alliance between the Hosokawa and Yamana families made it possible to replace Mochikuni (who died of chagrin in 1445), it did not last long. Before the alliance broke down, however, opposition to the naming of Yoshimasa as shogun had melted away.

Ashikaga Yoshimasa, the eighth Ashikaga shogun, was born in 1436, two years after his brother Yoshikatsu. The mother of both, Hino Shigeko, came from a family that claimed descent from the legendary Fujiwara no Kamatari (614–699).[13] If his brother had not died young, Yoshimasa probably would have entered Buddhist orders. Instead, at the age of seven, he became the head of the Ashikaga family, though he did not succeed to the office of shogun until after his *genbuku* ceremony in 1449.

The strongest influence in Yoshimasa's boyhood was exerted by his nurse, Imamairi no tsubone (d. 1459),[14] a member of the prominent Ōdachi family, which had served the shoguns as personal attendants from Yoshimitsu's day. Imamairi is said to have waited on Yoshimasa ever since he was in diapers and was credited with having transmitted to a weak-spirited boy something of her own impetuosity.

While Yoshimasa was still a minor, both his mother, Hino Shigeko, and his nurse, Imamairi, were accused of meddling in the government.[15] Undoubtedly both women at times attempted to gain personal advantage from their relationship to the future shogun, but much of their "meddling" may actually have consisted of nothing more than attempts to defend Yoshimasa from rapacious military governors.

A notable instance of Imamairi's "meddling" occurred in 1451. In that year, Yoshimasa dismissed Oda Toshihiro as acting military governor of Owari and replaced him with his brother, a man who had earlier displeased Ashikaga Yoshinori. As soon as Yoshimasa's decision became known, it was vociferously attacked by the shogunal deputy and by Hino Shigeko, who declared that the dismissal might well lead to disastrous consequences. Yoshimasa refused to back down. It is surprising that the young shogun, only fifteen years old, entertained such strong views about who should be acting military governor of Owari. Shigeko was told that he had made this decision because he was completely under Imamairi's influence. Enraged because her opinion had not been asked, she announced her intention of leaving the Muromachi Palace. Various daimyos sympathized with Shigeko, and in the end Yoshimasa, unable to withstand their pressure, had no choice but to rescind the order replacing the acting military governor. Although her victory did not diminish Shigeko's hatred for Imamairi, it taught Yoshimasa the limits of his power.

Yoshimasa's education was in the traditional mode. It officially began in 1446, when he was ten, with a customary "first reading," probably from the Confucian classic *The Book of Filial Piety*; but it undoubtedly had begun much earlier, along lines considered suitable for a future shogun, including the study of both literary and martial arts. Yoshimasa showed conspicuously less interest in

sports than in literature and the arts. As a necessary accomplishment for a gentleman, he learned how to compose *waka* and studied calligraphy under the founder of the Asukai school.[16]

Yoshimasa's education was mainly in the hands of the Ise family.
It had long been the custom of the imperial family to entrust an
emperor's children to a retainer for their upbringing. (This
remained true even of Emperor Meiji's children.) The shogun, too,
in imitation of the imperial family, normally asked a retainer to
take charge of his children during their formative years. Yoshimasa
thus was educated initially by Ise Sadakuni, a man well versed in
martial traditions. The Ise family was of high court rank and traced
its ancestry back to the Heian period. In the Kamakura period,
members of the family had served as governors of the province of
Ise, from which they took their family name. Ever since Yoshimitsu's time, the Ise family had served in the hereditary office of
administrative deputy (*mandokoro shitsuji*).

The role played by the Ise family—in particular, Ise Sadachika
(1417–1473)—in Yoshimasa's education accounted for its prominent role during his reign as shogun. The relations between Yoshimasa and Sadachika were particularly close, with Yoshimasa referring to Sadachika, nineteen years his senior, as "father."[17]

In the first month of 1455, drawings of three people were put up
at a conspicuous place in the capital along with the inscription
"The government of late has been run by three demons—Oima,
Arima, and Karasuma." Each of the these names ends with the syl-
lable *ma*, which has the same pronunciation as the word for
"demon."[18] The three "demons" were said to have induced Yoshimasa to issue decrees that benefited themselves.

Accusations of this nature, especially against Imamairi, continued to be recorded in diaries of the time. An entry for the first
month of 1459 in *Hekizan nichiroku*, the diary of the Zen priest
Unsen Taikyoku (1422–1478?), describes the extraordinary extent
of Imamairi's influence on ministers of state. Taikyoku referred to

Imamairi as Yoshimasa's "favorite mistress." This has given rise to speculation about whether she was his nurse or his mistress; perhaps she was both. It would not have been surprising if Imamairi, having reared the boy Yoshimasa to early manhood, also inducted him into the ways of love, even though she was more than ten years his senior. In any case, Yoshimasa was precocious: by the time of his marriage, he already had had numerous affairs and was the father of three daughters.[19]

Whatever Yoshimasa's relations with Imamairi may have been, there was no possibility that she would become his consort. Once again, a bride for a shogun was chosen from the Hino family, and in the eighth month of 1455 Yoshimasa and Hino Tomiko were married. The groom was twenty and the bride, fifteen. To celebrate the occasion, the emperor bestowed on Yoshimasa the court title of Commander of the Right Palace Guards.

Hino Shigeko was doubtless pleased to have her grandniece chosen as the shogun's bride. Now her main problem was how to get rid of Imamairi. Nothing indicates that Yoshimasa was in love with his bride, but he definitely seems to have lost interest in the aging Imamairi, though she was still a person of consequence at the shogun's court. In order to keep Yoshimasa's affections from wandering too far from herself, Imamairi had introduced into his bedroom a young niece (or cousin?) called Sanko, who in 1455 bore Yoshimasa a daughter.

In 1459 Tomiko bore a son who died almost at once. Rumors had it that Imamairi had suborned mountain ascetics (*shugenja*) to pray for the infant's death.[20] Hino Shigeko, sure that a curse had been responsible, convinced Yoshimasa that Imamairi was to blame. In a rage over the loss of his first son, Yoshimasa ordered Kyōgoku Mochikiyo to arrest Imamairi and escort her to banishment on an island in Lake Biwa. Four days later, she was dead. Some sources indicate that she was put to death by drowning, but most chroniclers of the time state that she learned while on the way to exile that a sentence of death had been passed on her and cheated the executioner by committing *seppuku*, proof that a woman was capable of the traditional samurai form of suicide.[21]

After Imamairi's death, both Tomiko and Shigeko suffered from nightmares in which her ghost appeared to torment them. Tomiko's slow and painful recovery from the stillbirth was blamed on Imamairi's fierce resentment over having been made the victim of a false charge of witchcraft. In 1463, when Hino Shigeko was suffering from a serious illness, she had memorial services conducted for Imamairi, believing that the illness had been caused by her defeated enemy. Years later, in 1480, when her younger son lost the sight in one eye, Tomiko attributed it to Imamairi's curse and built a Shinto shrine in Kyoto where Imamairi was the chief figure of worship.[22]

After Imamairi's death, there was no question but that Hino Tomiko was the most influential of the women surrounding Yoshimasa. Among the men, Ise Sadachika exercised the greatest power. Sadachika succeeded to the office of administrative secretary in 1460 and soon demonstrated his ability. It is true that the shogunate did not enjoy the prosperity of former reigns, but Sadachika had the necessary business acumen to preserve the structure from collapsing for want of funds. Realizing that Yoshimasa was unlikely to be of assistance in keeping the shogunate solvent, Sadachika encouraged him to indulge in physical pleasures, in this way keeping him from interfering in state business.

Sadachika was less successful in keeping Tomiko under control. In 1478 new barriers were erected at the seven gateways to the capital, this time for the announced purpose of raising funds for repairing the Tsuchimikado Palace. However, a distinguished priest wrote in his diary that he had heard from Sōgi, the great *renga* poet, that this was a pretext: all the money went to Tomiko, who lent it at high interest rates to daimyos impoverished by the long war.[23] Tomiko is traditionally reputed to have been inordinately fond of money. Indeed, it was rumored that a major part of the shogunate's income found its way into her hands. One recent scholar, seeking to rehabilitate Tomiko's reputation, wrote, "Tomiko had no fault worth mentioning. She is said to have been fond of money, but she was not stingy. When there was money to be given, she gave it unstintingly."[24]

This gallant defense of a woman who was notorious for her avarice does not make us forget accounts by Tomiko's contemporaries who expressed their conviction that her greed was unbounded. The celebrated priest-poet Ikkyū left several *kanshi* in which he indirectly accused Tomiko of being like Yang Kuei-fei, the woman whose beauty had caused an infatuated Chinese emperor to lose his throne. Among the poems are the following:

> Treasures and money are a source of betrayal;
> An elegant woman should not desire such things.
> The danger within Japan is painful to contemplate;
> The hearts of loyal ministers are tangled like threads.[25]

> Smoke and dust rose over the whole country
> Only for the east wind last night to blow them away.
> But calamity will strike a beautiful woman once again;
> Remember the spring at Ma-wei and repent of your splendor.[26]

The poems criticized Hino Tomiko by likening her to Yang Kuei-fei, for Ikkyū could not attack her openly. He warns her that even if her beauty enabled her to amass wealth, her glory would be short-lived. Tomiko probably was beautiful when she was young, but the face of her portrait statue indicates that determination, rather than beauty, characterized her features in middle age.

3

Ashikaga Yoshimasa, a boy of thirteen, was proclaimed shogun in 1449. He no doubt had been
informed how his father had been murdered and
what struggles for power had ensued. Perhaps these
circumstances inhibited him from exercising his
privileges as shogun, but in his youth he apparently
entertained ambitions of restoring the grandeur of
the shogunate during the reigns of his grandfather
and father. To this end, he revived customs that had
fallen into disuse, even some that may seem to us of
little intrinsic importance. In 1460, for example, he
ordered that one gate to the shogunate buildings be
closed to all but vehicles and riders on official business. The sole reason for this order was that such
had been the practice in Yoshinori's time. Again,

Yoshimasa commanded that documents issued in Yoshinori's name be investigated in order to ascertain exactly where on each document his signet (*kaō*) was affixed; he had decided to affix his own signet at the same place. In such instances, the reasons why these practices had originated were irrelevant. All that mattered was restoring these tiny fragments of a past that seemed more glorious than the present.

Yoshimasa's efforts to restore the past were not confined to trivia. Although he is usually pictured by historians as a man incapable of action and indifferent to infringements on the shogunate's authority, in his youth he made determined attempts to control the military governors. He failed, largely because of personal weaknesses, but also because conditions at the time did not permit the shogun to wield the authority of a Yoshimitsu or Yoshinori.[1]

Today Yoshimasa is generally better known for his failings than for his modest attempts to act the part of a shogun. His faults, however, were intimately related to aesthetic preferences that were his major contribution to Japanese culture. Although his passion for building palaces led to immense debts and desperate, usually ill-conceived attempts to raise money to pay the bills, this passion also fostered the development of a distinctive new architecture. To the people of the time, the great expenditure of money was more obvious than the artistic contribution. In 1458, the same year that his costly renovation of the shogun's palace (Karasuma-dono) was completed, Yoshimasa decided that it should be moved to the site of the old Muromachi Palace, probably out of nostalgia for the days of Yoshimitsu, who had built his palace there. His wishes were obeyed, despite the cost. The altered construction was carried out with the utmost lavishness.

One scheme for raising money to pay for these new buildings and Yoshimasa's other extravagances was to grant *tokusei*, which annulled debts, on condition that the beneficiaries return one-tenth of the sum to the *bakufu*. The first such *buichi tokusei*, as it was called, was promulgated in 1454. It did not take long for clever men to find ways of circumventing the shogunate's regulations, and the expected funds failed to materialize. In 1457, after there had been uprisings against usurers in various parts of the country, the shogunate issued another kind of *tokusei*, this one promising relief to the lenders, provided that they paid the shogunate one-fifth of the sums lent. It also prescribed punishment for both borrowers and lenders in the event that they colluded.

A second plan for raising money, more effective but even more unpopular, called for the establishment of new barriers on the roads leading into the capital, at which fees would be collected for those wishing to pass. The necessity of paying these fees so angered people that they staged rebellions. The shogunate responded by abolishing the barriers, only to erect new ones in 1459 at the seven entrances to Kyoto.[2] Although the barriers brought in income, it was not enough to rescue the shogunate from a seemingly irreversible process of decline and decay.

Yoshimasa lacked the martial disposition essential to the chief officer of a military government. For all his profound interest in nō and other arts, Yoshimasa's grandfather, Ashikaga Yoshimitsu, had been a warrior by temperament, but Yoshimasa aspired to become not an invincible general but a second Genji. Handsome, sensitive, and seemingly irresistible to women, he was well qualified for the role. His tastes were those of an aristocrat rather than of a samurai. A contemporary Zen monk described him as "mild and gentle" (*onkyō wajun*),[3] admirable qualities in themselves, but not those most needed in a military ruler.

At least while he was young, Yoshimasa felt concern for the welfare of his subjects. His mildness and gentleness may have inspired his many gifts to relieve the suffering caused by the terrible famine of 1459.[4] Perhaps his generous impulses were abetted by an otherworldly source. In 1461, as one account informs us, Yoshimasa had a dream in which his father, Yoshinori, imposing in formal robes, informed Yoshimasa that he was suffering now for the crimes he, Yoshinori, had committed while he was alive; but because he had also performed virtuous acts, he expected to be reborn as a shogun. The apparition commanded Yoshimasa to give alms to victims of the famine, saying this would alleviate the pains he was enduring in hell. Yoshimasa at once directed a shogunate official to make suitable donations.[5]

Other anecdotes suggest that Yoshimasa recognized the great gap between the affluence of his own life and the misery in which the mass of the people lived. For example, in the autumn of 1461 when he went to view the colored maple leaves at the Saihō-ji (the temple familiarly known as the Moss Temple), he asked an attendant why it was that although the colored leaves were so glorious, the houses in the city around them looked so miserable. He wondered whether it might be because taxes were excessive.[6]

Such moments of expressed concern for the welfare of the common people grew increasingly rare. Although he was aware of the terrible suffering caused by the famine, Yoshimasa seems not to have considered reducing his expenditures in order to bring relief to those who were starving. During the worst of the famine, he did not forgo such pleasures as admiring the plum and cherry blossoms at famous sites and attending performances of nō. Nor did he hesitate to spend vast sums of money for rebuilding the Muromachi Palace, known as the Palace of Flowers (Hana no gosho) because its extensive gardens were filled with flowers.

Worse still, when he realized that he had been unsuccessful in his attempts to restore the shogunate to its former glory, he led a life of the utmost dissipation, seeking to forget his failure by indulging in women and drink. By this time, his personal efforts on behalf of the country and the people had dwindled to nothingness. He was shielded from criticism, however, by the sycophants with whom he surrounded himself and by the pervasiveness of luxury among the members of the military class, especially the high-ranking officers, who accepted Yoshimasa's unrestrained extravagance as normal.

The famine that began in 1459 continued for three years. Prolonged drought was followed by torrential rains, and the rains in turn were followed by a plague of locusts that devoured what few crops had survived. The famine affected much of the country, from the capital in Kyoto all the way to the provinces facing the Inland Sea and the Japan Sea. Many people starved in the countryside, and more perished on the roads as they desperately struggled to reach the capital in the hopes of finding food. Death seemed to be omnipresent except in the Palace of Flowers. An entry for the sixteenth day of the third month (April 9) of 1460 from *Hekizan nichiroku*, the diary of the Zen priest Unsen Taikyoku, contrasts the misery of the starving poor with the arrogance of the rich:

When the sun went down I set out for home, and as I was passing Rokujō I saw an old woman with a child in her arms. She called the child's name repeatedly, then began to wail. I looked and saw that the child was already dead. The mother, still wailing, collapsed on the ground. People standing nearby asked her where she came from. She said, "I've come all the way from Kawachi. We've had a terrible drought for three years, and the rice plants didn't so much as sprout. The district officials are cruel and greedy. They demand a lot of money in taxes and show no mercy. If you don't pay, they kill you. That's why I had to run away to another province. I was hoping to earn food by begging. But I couldn't get anything to give my baby. I'm starving and I'm worn out, heart and soul. I can't take any more."

When she had finished speaking, she again choked with great sobs. I took from my wallet what spare money I had and gave it to her, saying, "Take this money and hire a man to bury the child. I'm going back to my cell where, with help from the Three Treasures and the Five Commandments, I shall choose a Buddhist name for the child and offer prayers for his salvation." The child's mother was greatly comforted.

While I was still humbly mulling over her sad story, I encountered a group of noblemen out to admire the blossoms. They were escorted by several thousand mounted men, and servants and followers swarmed around them. These gentlemen acted as if they were so superior that nobody could compare with them. Some sneered at the people in the streets; others swore at the menials in the path of their horses; others laughingly stole blossoms; others, drunkenly singing, drew their swords; others still, having vomited food and drink and being unable to walk, lay on the roadside. There were many such sights, and whoever saw them was appalled. Anyone who happened to run into these people was terrified and ran away, intimidated by their high rank.[7]

At the time, of course, such criticism was not openly expressed, but in somewhat later writings the arrogant insensitivity of the nobles to the suffering of the poor was often cited as a cause of the Ōnin War:

Was it perhaps a portent that a great disturbance was about to break out? The nobles and military alike were greatly given to luxury, and in the towns and countryside, and even in remote regions, quite ordinary people indulged in display. The opulence of the great houses and the suffering of the masses were beyond description. This caused the masses anguish and distress, and they cried out like the people of Hsia in protest against the outrages of King Chieh: "Who will perish today? Perhaps it will be the both of us." If there were loyal subjects at this time, why did they not come forth with remonstrances? Instead, people displayed an attitude of "if the country is going to break, let it break, if society is to perish, let it perish." They acted as if they were indifferent to what happened to others; as long as they themselves had wealth and rank, all they thought of was shining more brilliantly than anyone else.[8]

Diaries describe how the stench from the corpses clogging the Kamo River pervaded the entire capital. When Taikyoku stood on the Shijō Bridge and looked down into the water, the river looked to him like a hilly landscape of bodies.[9] He mentioned the case of a monk who had placed slips of wood (*sotoba*) on the heads of some 82,000 corpses, hoping this would bring them salvation. Many more people died in the surrounding countryside than in the city itself. Cases of cannibalism were reported.

Even though the city reeked from the bodies clogging the Kamo River, Yoshimasa went ahead with the rebuilding of the Muromachi Palace. He also planned to construct another, entirely new palace. According to traditional accounts, the only person who dared reprove this seeming callousness was Emperor Go-Hanazono, who in 1460 sent Yoshimasa a quatrain in Chinese. A chronicle composed some years later described the circumstances leading to the composition of the poem:

In the same year [1461] there was a great famine throughout the land, beginning in the spring. An epidemic of many diseases was also prevalent. Two-thirds of the people died of starvation, and skeletons filled the streets. Nobody passed but was moved to pity. But the shogun at the time, Ashikaga Yoshimasa, had built the Palace of Flowers in the second month of 1459 and doted on the place. Every day he employed people to create [gardens with] mountains, water, plants, and trees, laying out streams and stones. Showing no pity for those who suffered from hunger, he made plans to build still another new palace. At this time the emperor, learning of the plan, sent a poem of his own composition to the shogun:

> Survivors scrabble for fern shoots on Mount Shou-yang[10]
> Everywhere people have shut their doors and chained their
>   bamboo gates.
> Poetic inspiration turns sour at the height of spring;
> For whom does the whole city burgeon red and green?[11]

After reading the poem, the shogun is said to have felt so ashamed that he ordered a halt to the construction of the new palace. People rejoiced, thinking that the lord had acted like a lord and the vassal like a vassal.[12]

Even if Yoshimasa felt shame when he recognized the sarcasm behind the poem—the emperor implied that only the shogun had the leisure to enjoy the spring—it did not keep him from rebuilding the Muromachi Palace. Moreover, when Emperor Go-Hanazono visited this palace soon after his abdication in 1464, he expressed delight over its many elaborate and beautiful features; he was far from condemning the prodigious expense. The poem attributed to the emperor also failed to stop another construction begun at this time, the Takakura Palace, which Yoshimasa built for his mother. Indeed, the story of the poem with which the emperor rebuked the shogun was probably invented by a chronicler.[13]

Frustrated in his attempts to display the authority of earlier shoguns, Yoshimasa may have decided about this time to abdicate in order to devote himself entirely to aesthetic pleasures. He could not resign, however, until he had a successor. Even a child would have been acceptable, but Yoshimasa had no sons: Hino Tomiko had not conceived since Imamairi's witchcraft allegedly prevented the safe delivery of her first child. Finally Yoshimasa decided on a plan of persuading his younger half brother, Ashikaga Yoshimi (1439–1491), who had become a Tendai monk as a boy of four, to return to the laity as his designated successor.

Yoshimi was extremely reluctant to leave Buddhist orders.

Return to the laity, he said, was unthinkable. He also feared that if he accepted Yoshimasa's proposal, he might be displaced as Yoshimasa's heir if Yoshimasa had a son of his own.

In order to relieve this anxiety, Yoshimasa promised that even if he had a son, the son would be placed as an infant in Buddhist orders and there would be no change in the succession. He swore in writing by the gods of heaven and earth, both great and small, that he would abide by these words.[14] Having received this assurance, Yoshimi returned to the laity in 1464 and was recognized as the adopted son of Yoshimasa and Hino Tomiko. He was given a palace, appointed to the fifth court rank, and began to frequent society, often in the company of his new father and mother.[15]

Although Yoshimasa now had a successor, he did not retire from office as he had planned, perhaps because he had been informed that Tomiko was with child. In the summer of 1465, the country rejoiced to learn that Tomiko had given birth to a boy.[16] She now bitterly regretted her husband's solemn promise that Yoshimi (whom she thought of with contempt) would be his successor and sought to find some way to have her son replace him. She secretly sent word to Yamana Sōzen, the most powerful of the military governors, asking him to place her son under his protection. She explained in her letter that having been granted a child at the advanced age of thirty, she could not bear to have him taken from her and put in a temple where his head would be shaved and he would be dressed in black robes.

When Sōzen read Tomiko's letter, he reasoned that if Yoshimi succeeded to the post of shogun he would certainly favor Hosokawa Katsumoto, who had acted like a father to him, and that this would be disadvantageous to the Yamana family. Although Sōzen foresaw the likelihood of conflict between his allies and those of Katsumoto, this did not deter him, for a war would give him an opportunity to destroy his rivals. He told Tomiko that he would accept her request.[17]

This was the immediate cause of the Ōnin War, during which the Yamana family supported Yoshihisa, the son of Tomiko, against Yoshimi, who was supported by the Hosokawa. In the first paragraph of *Ōnin ki*, the author blames Yoshimasa, and especially the women around Yoshimasa, for the turmoil into which the country was plunged by the war:

> The fault lay with his lordship, the Shogun Yoshimasa, who was the seventh shogun after Takauji. Instead of entrusting the affairs of the country to his worthy ministers, Yoshimasa governed solely by the wishes of such ignorant wives and nuns as Lady Tomiko, Lady Shigeko, and Kasuga-no-tsubone. Yet these women did not know the difference between right and wrong and were ignorant of public office and the ways of government. Orders were given freely from the muddle of drinking parties and lustful pleasure-seeking. Bribery was freely dispensed.[18]

Blaming national misfortune on the influence of women was not new. The woes of Chinese emperors were frequently attributed to women who "overturned the state" (*keisei*), and in Japan the dangers implicit in the emperor's passionate love for Kiritsubo is evoked on the first page of *The Tale of Genji*:

> His court looked with very great misgivings upon what seemed a reckless infatuation. In China such an unreasoning passion had been the undoing of an emperor and had spread turmoil throughout the land. As the resentment grew, the example of Yang Kuei-fei was the one most frequently cited against the lady.[19]

The behavior of Yoshimasa's mother, Hino Shigeko, and his wife, Hino Tomiko, was held up by diarists of the time as an extreme example of the pernicious influence of women. It was to comfort Shigeko, who had been distressed at not being allowed to visit the beautiful garden of the Saihō-ji (because women were strictly prohibited inside this temple), that in 1462 Yoshimasa built at the new Takakura Palace a replica of the Saihō-ji garden. Even though this was an act of filial piety, diarists of the time did not praise Yoshimasa's decision to build a luxurious palace, decorated by the finest artists, immediately after a famine.

Yoshimasa's seeming inability to control Tomiko's greed earned him the contempt of modern writers, who share the dismay of the author of *Ōnin ki* regarding women who meddle in government affairs. However, the outstanding scholar of the age, Ichijō Kaneyoshi (1402–1481), in "Sayo no nezame" (Waking at Night), a work written in about 1473, expressed quite a different opinion about the role of women in government:

> In general, women follow their parents when they are young, their husbands as adults, and their sons in old age and, for this reason, do not make a name for themselves in the world. They are expected to be gentle and pliant. But this land of Japan is called *wakoku* [land of harmony and peace] and, for that reason, should be governed by women. The great goddess Amaterasu was a woman, and the empress Jingū, who was the mother of the bodhisattva Hachiman [the god of war], attacked and pacified the kingdoms of Shiragi and Kudara [in Korea] and founded this Land of Reed Plains. . . . Therefore, no one should be looked down on because she is a woman. In ancient times many female emperors augustly ruled. Even now, if there were a truly august woman, she should rule the nation.[20]

Kaneyoshi seems to have been currying favor with Tomiko when he wrote this, but perhaps he really believed that women were particularly qualified to rule Japan, despite the many examples of disaster that were conventionally attributed to their influence.

Regardless of whether Tomiko's influence was beneficial to the nation, it can hardly be doubted that her intense desire to have her own son become the next shogun, even if this obliged Yoshimasa to violate his solemn vow to Yoshimi, was a cause of the outbreak of war. Many other causes would be listed in a political or economic history of the age. Succession disputes in the Hatakeyama and Shiba families served to polarize the Yamana and the Hosokawa, the two main combatants during the ensuing war. There also were negative causes: if the shogunate had been led by a strong shogun like Yoshimitsu or Yoshinori, the war probably would not have taken place.

The most unusual feature of the war as it developed was the almost total lack of involvement by the shogun (and the emperor) in a war that destroyed the city of Kyoto, where both remained during the ten years of warfare. Although the chronicler of *Ōnin ki* was biased against Tomiko and other women of the shogun's court, he did not neglect to blame men for the outbreak of war. Yoshimasa, of course, was rebuked for both his extravagance and his fatal lack of leadership. Ise Sadachika, Yoshimasa's longtime mentor, who was treated even more harshly, was denounced as a corrupt official whose judgments at the Administrative Headquarters (Mandokoro), over which he presided, favored whoever paid him the largest bribe.

Sadachika's "craving for pleasures of the flesh" and "lustful affairs" were also prominently mentioned in *Ōnin ki* as typifying the corruption of the times. It is ironic that this man should now be best known for the pious "maxims" he prepared to guide his "stupid son." These teachings, with which Yoshimasa was certainly familiar, emphasized the importance of worshiping Buddha and the Japanese gods but also dealt with such worldly matters as the correct behavior for an official, the courtesy appropriate to dealing with people regardless of class, and the desirable artistic accomplishments for a gentleman. Naturally, Sadachika's maxims say nothing about the pleasures of lust or of bribe taking, but Yoshimasa may have been influenced in this respect by what he knew of

Sadachika's private life, quite apart from the maxims. Sadachika's influence in forming the character of the young shogun could hardly be said to have been beneficial. It certainly did not prepare Yoshimasa for the role of a leader in times of war.

The conflict that became known as the Ōnin War began with the dispute between two warring factions within the Hatakeyama family over the succession to the office of shogunal deputy. The dispute curiously paralleled the division within the shogun's family: having failed to produce a male heir, Hatakeyama Mochikuni adopted his nephew and solemnly promised to make Masanaga his heir. Not long afterward, one of Mochikuni's concubines gave birth to a son, Yoshinari. Mochikuni became extremely fond of Yoshinari, and when he retired in 1450 he attempted to make him his heir, despite the binding promise to Masanaga. Both men had powerful backers. In 1454 Mochikuni secured a directive from the shogun confirming Yoshinari's succession as head of the family, but soon afterward Yoshimasa took a dislike to Yoshinari and refused to recognize his claims. His irresolute actions undoubtedly contributed to the tension between the two factions. Fighting broke out between the supporters of the rival cousins and continued sporadically for a decade until Masanaga returned in triumph to the capital in 1464 and was proclaimed as the shogunal deputy.[21]

This should have ended the dispute, but in fact it dragged on and eventually became intertwined with the dispute between Yoshimi and Yoshihisa and with a similar dispute over the headship of the Shiba family. It is extremely difficult to remember the events and names of all who were involved, but the most important fact is that the Hosokawa and Yamana families, which had been allied by marriage, had grown apart and were backing opposing factions.

At this time, the Yamana family, whose fortunes were rising, supported the defeated Hatakeyama Yoshinari and secured Yoshimasa's permission for him to return to the capital. Yoshimasa was apparently so intimidated by Yamana Sōzen that he canceled

Masanaga's appointment as shogunal deputy. Sōzen, confident of his control over the shogun, demanded next that Hosokawa Katsumoto cease to support Masanaga, and Yoshimasa, under Sōzen's influence, sent a warning to this effect. Katsumoto's response was to summon troops to his mansion to prepare for war. Yoshimasa, alarmed by the likelihood of war, ordered, in an atypical show of firmness, both Yamana and Hosokawa to stay out of the Hatakeyama dispute.

Hosokawa Katsumoto obeyed the shogun's order, but Yamana Sōzen secretly sent assistance to Yoshinari. Masanaga, who had reports that Katsumoto's support was weakening, decided to attack, hoping that this would rouse Katsumoto into action. On learning that Masanaga had burned down his own house as a sign that the course he was about to take was irreversible, Yoshimasa feared that he might occupy the nearby imperial palace. He hastily moved the emperor and retired emperor to safety in the Palace of Flowers.

The Ōnin War[22] broke out at dawn on the eighteenth day of the first month of the second year of Bunshō, or February 22, 1467.[23] The place was the Kami Goryō Shrine to the north of Kyoto, not far from the imperial palace. Fighting began in the afternoon, but as the day came to a close it was still not clear which side had won. Masanaga appealed to Katsumoto for reinforcements, but Katsumoto, obeying Yoshimasa's order to stay out of the dispute, did not respond. Sensing defeat, Masanaga asked Katsumoto for a gift of saké, intending to drink a farewell cup, but Katsumoto sent an arrow instead, meaning that Masanaga should fight gallantly to the death. Masanaga was defeated and fled. Fifty or sixty of his men were killed. Others took refuge in the Shōkoku-ji, where they committed suicide the next morning.

The fighting at the Goryō Shrine was on a small scale. Masanaga probably had only about five hundred men and Yoshinari, about a thousand. The Yamana had helped Yoshinari, but

Katsumoto studiously avoided violating Yoshimasa's command, perhaps out of respect for the shogunate, but more likely because his forces were not yet ready. The Yamana forces exulted in the victory, and it seemed that the fighting was over. The emperor and retired emperor moved back to the imperial palace. The nobles decided that the reign-name Bunshō had been the cause of the warfare and, praying for peace, changed it to Ōnin. The illusion that peace had been restored did not last long, however. Having decided that it was useless to try to reach a political settlement with the Yamana, Katsumoto expedited his preparations for war.

4

Although the Ōnin War ostensibly was fought to decide whether Ashikaga Yoshimi (Yoshimasa's half brother) or Ashikaga Yoshihisa (his son) would succeed Yoshimasa as shogun, it was essentially a struggle between the Hosokawa and Yamana families for control of Japan. The fighting dragged on for ten years. It was largely confined to Kyoto and resulted in the almost complete destruction of the only large city in Japan. Accounts written by people who remembered the appearance of Kyoto at the height of its glory described their shock when returning after the war, they saw how terribly the city had been ravaged. Of course, many cities all over the world have since been shattered by street fighting or bombing, but if the buildings are of brick or stone, at least hollow shells remain as reminders that a city once stood there. In Kyoto, however, the buildings were made of wood, and nothing was left after the fighting except the occasional storehouse with earthen walls and a few temples that had miraculously escaped the fires. The desolation was almost total.

If one examines a map of Kyoto showing the sites of the principal buildings before the outbreak of war, one cannot fail to be struck by how close together they were. The distance separating the main residences of the Yamana and Hosokawa clans could be walked in minutes, and from either of these mansions to the shogun's Palace of Flowers and the imperial palace was a bare twenty minutes' walk. Despite the closeness of the headquarters of the warring factions, the Hosokawa clan was known as the Eastern Army, and the Yamana clan was called the Western Army, as if they were situated in quite different parts of Japan. The headquarters were given these names simply because they were somewhat to the east or the west of the center of the city.[1] Later, the terms acquired another meaning: the Yamana clan drew its strength from the provinces of western Honshū (as well as of Shikoku and most of Kyūshū), whereas the Hosokawa soldiers were mainly from eastern Japan.

There was a lull in the fighting after the first encounter at the Kami Goryō Shrine between factions of the Hatakeyama family. On the third day of the third month (April 6), a great party was held at the shogun's palace to celebrate the annual spring festival. Some three thousand people attended, all dressed in magnificent robes and carrying swords decorated with gold and mother-of-pearl. The splendor of the gathering was so dazzling that some people wondered whether the expense might not bankrupt the country.

After offering their holiday greetings at the shogun's palace, the celebrants proceeded to the Imadegawa Palace of the shogun's half brother and designated successor, Yoshimi, to express their loyalty. But although Yamana Sōzen and many daimyos allied with the

Yamana took part in the festivities, the Hosokawa were conspicuous by their absence.[2] They were busy with day-and-night planning sessions and other preparations for war and could not spare
the time to attend a feast.

The decision of the Hosokawa to attack the Yamana seems to
have been precipitated by the plea made by the lay priest Jiken. In
the first month of 1467, when Hatakeyama Masanaga had begged
Hosokawa Katsumoto for help against his cousin Yoshinari, Jiken
had tearfully implored Katsumoto not to intervene. Now, once
again in tears, he begged quite the opposite, that Katsumoto avenge
the humiliating defeat that Masanaga had suffered because the
Hosokawa had failed to lend their support. Jiken urged Katsumoto
to wipe out the disgrace to the family name.[3]

Masanaga, who had been in hiding ever since his defeat by the
Yamana clan, at this point showed up at Katsumoto's camp, ready
for action. Soon troop commanders and men from many parts of
the country joined the sixty thousand vassals of imperial and
shogunal troops in Kyoto; Hosokawa Katsumoto could count on a
total of 161,500 mounted men. According to *Ōnin ki*, Yamana
Sōzen had only 116,000 riders at his disposal, but despite their
numerical inferiority, the Yamana men controlled six of the seven
approaches to the city.[4]

Fighting between the two clans erupted at dawn on the twenty-
sixth day of the fifth month (June 27) of 1467, when Hosokawa soldiers opened fire on Yamana forces. The engagement ended in a
minor victory for the Yamana, but a disproportionately large number of houses belonging to both sides were consumed in fires that
spread to many parts of the city. As yet, however, the shogunate was
not involved, and Yoshimasa's position was not known. He sent
messengers to both sides commanding them to stop the warfare.
But at the same time, he ordered Ise Sadachika to bring his forces
to Kyoto, an indication that he feared the fighting would not end
soon. Probably he foresaw that the shogunate would need rein-

forcements in the event of a major showdown between the Yamana
and Hosokawa clans.

Yoshimasa had earlier exiled Sadachika from the capital when he
discovered that he had falsely accused Yoshimi of plotting to seize
power, but he probably still considered Sadachika as his mentor
and hoped that he might save the country from all-out civil war. At
first Yoshimasa refused to take sides, but in the sixth month he clar-
ified his position by ordering Yoshimi and Katsumoto to attack the
Yamana clan.

Hino Tomiko and her brother, Hino Katsumitsu, who favored
the Yamana and opposed Yoshimi, strongly opposed this decision,
but Yoshimasa held firm and bestowed on Katsumoto the shogunal
banner to fly over his headquarters. Yoshimi, named as commanding general, opened the attack on the Western Army, now stigma-
tized as rebels. In a battle fought on the eighth day of the sixth
month, the Eastern Army was victorious. Supposing that this victory signified that the Western army had been crushed, Yoshimasa
sent a memorandum to its generals urging them to surrender.
Some obeyed and shifted their allegiance to the Eastern Army, and
others withdrew altogether from the fighting. Encouraged by
these defections, the Eastern Army attacked the residences of
major supporters of the Western Army. Huge fires were started
that gutted much of the city.

Advantage in the fighting seemed to be on the side of the
Hosokawa, but the Western Army held on, heartened by reports
that an army under the command of Ōuchi Masahiro would soon
arrive in the capital. On the twenty-third day of the eighth month,
Masahiro's army, said to be thirty thousand men strong, occupied
the Tōji and the southern part of the city, giving Yamada Sōzen's
army superiority at least for the moment. Katsumoto responded by
asking both Emperor Go-Tsuchimikado and Retired Emperor
Go-Hanazono to move to the Muromachi Palace, the seat of the
shogunate. Go-Tsuchimikado took with him the imperial regalia.

The Eastern Army could claim to be the emperor's troops,[5] but the reinforcements had made the Western Army stronger.

Ashikaga Yoshimi, who had valiantly fought against the Western Army, was worried by the apparent improvement in the Yamana clan's fortunes. He suspected that Yoshimasa might secretly be favoring the Yamana; Tomiko certainly was. He reasoned that if he gave further support to the Hosokawa, this might damage his relations with Yoshimasa and hurt his chances of succeeding him as shogun. Yoshimi therefore decided to remove himself temporarily from the scene of the fighting and to await further developments. He made his way to the foot of Mount Hiei, where his wife had taken refuge, and from there went on to Ise, where he accepted the hospitality of the provincial governor.

Yoshimasa was dismayed to learn of Yoshimi's flight. Regardless of Yoshimi's reasons for turning his back on the fighting, the effect was to make Yoshimasa, who up to this point (in keeping with his vow) had supported Yoshimi's candidacy as the next shogun, shift his support to the cause of his son, Yoshihisa.

A major battle of the Ōnin War was fought in the tenth month of 1467 between the Yamana and Hosokawa clans for possession of the Shōkoku-ji. This Zen temple, founded by Ashikaga Takauji, was of particular importance to the Ashikaga family. Because it was situated very close to the Palace of Flowers, the Yamana clan believed that occupying the temple would serve to drive a wedge between the palace and the Hosokawa residence. The fighting initially favored the Yamana, who had the covert help of a priest of the Shōkoku-ji who set fires inside the temple. Smoke from the burning buildings hovered over the shogun's palace, arousing fear of an imminent enemy attack.

In a state of panic, Tomiko and the other ladies of the shogun's household anxiously wondered how to escape, but Yoshimasa, unruffled by these fears and looking exactly as he always did, went on enjoying a drinking party. A retainer, sure that the impending battle would be his last, came before Yoshimasa to ask for a cup of saké from his hand, saying that it would be his reward for a lifetime of service and a keepsake to take to the afterworld. Yoshimasa complacently bestowed the desired cup of saké, which the man lifted reverently, saying, "The kindness of my lord this day will repay me for offering my hundred years of life." He went off and soon afterward was killed in the fighting. Yoshimasa remained undisturbed.[6]

Poems by the priest Ikkyū that were composed at this time describe the scenes of battle and destruction he witnessed. Although he never tired of condemning the falseness of the society in which he lived, he maintained his reverence for the imperial family and worried about its fate during the fighting. His reverence also induced him to attribute victories won by the Eastern Army to the virtue emanating from the court.[7] In his poem "After the Fire in the Capital," written some months after the Shōkoku-ji had been destroyed in the fire, he found hope in the survival of the imperial palace amid the devastation of the war:

> Cold ashes pile high in the streets of the capital.
> Only in the second month have flowers and spring
>   grasses sprouted.
> But the lovely palaces stand, untouched by events,
> And the emperor's envoy has brought a thousand
>   years of peace.[8]

His poem "Celebrating the Victory of the Imperial Forces over the Rebels on New Year's Day" exulted over the Eastern Army's victory in an attack staged at night on New Year's Day of the second year of Ōnin (1468):

> On New Year's day, after crushing the enemy,
> Everywhere men raised loud songs of triumph.
> A million soldiers of the imperial court
> And not one had lost so much as a single hair.[9]

Yoshimasa's feelings about the war were expressed quite differently, as in this *waka*:

hakanaku mo	Forlorn though the hope,
nao osamare to	Still I believe that somehow
omou kana	Peace will be restored.
kaku midaretaru	Although it is so confused,
yo woba itowade	I don't despair of the world.[10]

Yoshimasa's poem suggests he believed that the disturbance would go away even if he did nothing. His attitude recalls Fujiwara Teika's "Reports of disturbances and punitive expeditions fill one's ears, but I pay them no attention. The red banners and the expeditions against traitors are no concern of mine."[11] An expression of indifference to the commotion raised by ignorant soldiers was perhaps admissible in an aristocrat like Teika, but Yoshimasa was the shogun, the commander of those fighting on his side. His detachment made meaningless the loss of lives.

Haga Kōshirō, who was deeply aware of Yoshimasa's role in fostering Japanese culture, wrote,

> Yoshimasa, as a statesman, and especially as the shogun during an age of confusion whose vortex was the great upheaval of the Ōnin and Bunmei eras, was a total failure. He bears at least a part of the responsibility for the outbreak of the great conflict, and his political record could be described quite literally as a series of failures; there is no room to defend him.[12]

Yoshimasa undoubtedly realized that he was an incompetent shogun. When his confidants sent him a flattering memorial acclaiming him in extravagant terms as "father and mother to the people" and describing in glowing terms his success at quelling military disturbances, he replied that the praise was excessive and untrue to the facts, and he ordered them to correct the memorial. Haga believed that as a ruler, Yoshimasa was no more than a "robot" without independence of spirit or leadership, an irresponsible, self-abandoned "onlooker."[13]

With respect to the culture of his time, however, Yoshimasa displayed extraordinary leadership, and the culture of which he was a great patron lasted long after the battles of the Ōnin War had been forgotten. Yoshimasa would be remembered for his encouragement of aesthetic tastes that, transmitted to the Japanese people, became indispensable to their culture. When one speaks today of *Nihon no kokoro*—the soul of Japan—one is likely to be referring to elements of Japanese cultural preferences that were encouraged by Yoshimasa.

Yoshimasa's involvement in the Ōnin War was minimal. Although he could not have avoided feelings of apprehension when the flames engulfing the city of Kyoto approached his palace, he did nothing to terminate the warfare. The destruction was almost total, as Ikkyū's poem "On the Warfare of the Bunmei Era"[14] suggests:

> One burst of flame and the capital—gilt palaces and
>   how many mansions—
> Turns before one's eyes into a wasteland.
> The ruins, more desolate by the day, are autumnal.
> Spring breezes, peach and plum blossoms, soon become
>   dark.[15]

Casualties were heavy. Ikkyū's poem "Mourning Those Killed in Action" describes the battlefields:

> Demons with red faces, their hot blood aroused,
> Their fierce cries all but sundered heaven and earth.
> Now, defeated in battle, heads sliced from trunks,
> Their souls are doomed to eternal oblivion.[16]

The fighting finally ended in the eleventh month of 1477. The commander of the Western Army, Ōuchi Yoshihiro, losing interest in a meaningless conflict, set fire to his encampment and marched away from Kyoto along with his remaining generals.

During the ten years of the fighting, Yoshimasa, seemingly indifferent to the course of the war, devoted himself to cultivating the arts. He has been compared with Hui-tsung (1082–1135), the last emperor of the Sung dynasty and the founder of the first Chinese academy of painting.[17] One Western authority on Chinese history wrote about Hui-tsung, "Although neither a wise nor successful ruler, the Emperor was both a devoted patron of the arts and a painter of high rank himself. He lavished upon pictures and ceramics the care and attention which he denied to affairs of state."[18] Hui-tsung took refuge in the arts from the factional disputes at his court and the menace of invasion by uncivilized tribes. He consecrated himself to the pursuit of aesthetic elegance.

Almost everything written about Hui-tsung's taste and manner of life could be said equally about Yoshimasa, whose love of the arts enabled him to remain serene even when battles raged around him. Hui-tsung made an unfortunate alliance with a tribe of northern barbarians whom he judged to be the less dangerous of two tribes threatening China; but before long they turned on him, and he died an exile in Manchuria. Yoshimasa was spared this kind of humiliation by his refusal to become involved during the Ōnin War. Instead, his greatest failing—his incompetence as a military leader—was his salvation.

The culture to which Yoshimasa so greatly contributed is known today as Higashiyama, from the section of Kyoto where he built the retreat where he lived from 1483 to 1490. Yoshimasa obviously did not create the new culture single-handedly. Unlike Hui-tsung, he is not known today as a master of painting, calligraphy, and poetry, though he was highly competent in the latter two arts.[19] Rather, Yoshimasa's greatest gift was his exceptional ability to detect talent in other people and his readiness to employ them, regardless of their social station.

In creating a new culture after the end of the Ōnin War, Yoshimasa was helped by daimyos from the provinces who had acquired a taste for culture as the result of giving refuge during the war to poets and artists who had fled the capital. Yoshimasa was helped also by learned Zen monks whom he consulted less on religious than on aesthetic matters. Ever since he was a young man, long before the outbreak of the Ōnin War, he had been closely involved with artistically gifted monks. For example, when he was thinking of giving names to three small pavilions in the garden of the Takakura Palace, he asked Zuikei Shūhō, the outstanding poet-priest of the time, to recommend some suitable names. Zuikei immediately suggested several, but Yoshimasa rejected them. Two other learned priests joined Zuikei in poring over books of Chinese poetry and prose in search of appropriate phrases that might be used in naming the buildings. They came up with a number, but Yoshimasa still was not satisfied. He directed them to give names that more specifically alluded to the special features of the moon and the mountains as observed at the garden of the Saihō-ji, the model for the new garden. For fifty days, the priests continued to mull over names for the buildings until Yoshimasa, after having repeatedly rejected the names proposed by the priests, at last accepted three.

Next, Yoshimasa asked another learned priest, Kikei Shinzui, who was also a celebrated calligrapher, to inscribe the names, but he repeatedly found fault with the examples submitted—either the characters were the wrong size or the style of calligraphy did not please him. Kikei wrote the same characters again and again, until at last they accorded fully with Yoshimasa's taste. Next, the names of the pavilions, in Kikei's handwriting, were carved on wooden plaques that would be hung over the entrances to the pavilions. Yoshimasa gave minute directions on the depth of the carving and the colors to be used in decorating the characters. Finally, he gave orders concerning the angles at which the plaques would be hung.

Even though Yoshimasa had chosen the most qualified men for each of the various artistic tasks, he did not leave the execution of a plaque (or the planning of a building or garden) to professionals but insisted that each creation meet his own conception of beauty. At times this annoyed men who were confident of their artistic skill, but Yoshimasa did not yield. He never tired of giving directions concerning the effects he desired. Many people—ranging from daimyos, Zen priests, rich merchants, and hermits all the way down to outcasts—participated in creating the Higashiyama culture, but ultimate guidance was provided by Yoshimasa, especially after construction started on his retreat.

Yoshimasa's aesthetic preferences were clearly revealed in the works he chose for his collection of Chinese paintings. He favored ink painters of the Southern Sung and Yüan periods, especially Ma Yüan, Hsia Kuei, and Li T'ang. These painters, all members of the academy founded by Emperor Hui-tsung, were especially popular in Japan, as we know from the large number of their paintings imported in the thirteenth and fourteenth centuries. Works by Chinese Zen masters like Mu Ch'i and Liang K'ai were rated higher in Japan than in China. Japanese painters, many of them Zen priests, initially copied the works of the Chinese masters more or less slavishly but gradually made the imported styles their own.

The greatest Japanese painter of the Higashiyama era was undoubtedly Sesshū (1420–1506), though he did not work in Kyoto because of the prolonged warfare.[20] Many other painters of importance created works of art for Yoshimasa, notably Kanō Masanobu (ca. 1434–ca. 1530), the founder of the Kanō school.

The Higashiyama taste, though its creation was chiefly indebted to the shogun (rather than to the emperor or members of the nobility), was aristocratic. It was typified by the Silver Pavilion (Ginkaku-ji), a nickname that implicitly contrasted its simple, subdued elegance with the brilliance of Yoshimitsu's Golden Pavilion (Kinkaku-ji). The Golden Pavilion was coated with shining gold leaf, but there was nothing silvery about the Silver Pavilion. Instead, the differences between the two buildings were symbolized by their names: Yoshimitsu's unconventional and sometimes even vulgar taste was symbolized by the glitter of gold, whereas Yoshimasa preferred the austerity of Chinese ink paintings to more obviously artistic effects. And because gold is more precious than silver, the Silver Pavilion suggests a decline in the fortunes of the shogun and of all Japan, even though the unadorned beauty of Yoshimasa's pavilion is closer to the hearts of the Japanese today than is Yoshimitsu's palatial temple.

Although the Gold and Silver Pavilions differed enormously, both were profoundly indebted to Chinese examples. The admiration of China displayed by the shoguns of the Muromachi period from Yoshimitsu's time on verged on idolatry. But when the Ashikaga shoguns renewed official trade relations with China after a lapse of centuries, the object was profit rather than the acquisition of culture. Takauji encouraged trade with China in the hopes of making huge profits, and he was not disappointed. In 1342 a ship sent to China with Japanese wares returned loaded with cash.[21] Takauji's ostensible purpose in promoting this trade with China was to raise money for completing the Tenryū-ji, a temple he had founded at the request of the Zen master Musō Soseki. Ships sent to China, then ruled by the Yüan (or Mongol) dynasty, were accordingly known as Tenryū-ji ships.

The early years of the Ming dynasty, after the Mongols were expelled from China, corresponded to the age of Ashikaga Yoshimitsu. Emperor Hung-wu, the founder of the Ming dynasty, sent three missions to Japan. The first announced his enthronement and his taking Great Ming as the name of his dynasty.[22] Hung-wu was attempting to bolster the prestige of his regime by persuading neighboring countries to acknowledge that they were tributaries of China.

Hung-wu's second mission to Japan carried an imperial rescript stating his grave concern about the raids by Japanese pirates on coastal cities.[23] He threatened the Japanese: "If you insist on committing robbery and piracy, We shall order Our fleet to sail to the different islands to arrest each of the outlaws and shall proceed into the land to bind their kings with ropes." He demanded that the Japanese declare their loyalty to China; otherwise, they should expect war.[24]

Hung-wu's missions, beginning with the first (in the eleventh month of 1368) were intercepted by Prince Kanenaga (d. 1383), a son of Go-Daigo and leader of Southern Court supporters who had not yet been subdued by Yoshimitsu. Kanenaga probably never saw the first, friendly letter from Hung-wu and was therefore annoyed by the harsh rescript. The third letter, sent to Japan in 1370, stated in conclusion,

If a small country of barbarians, alien to Us, is not content with its lot and deliberately violates the way of Heaven by frequently coming to create disturbances, this inevitably incurs the hatred of spirits and men, and can hardly be tolerated by Heaven. Would it not be well for you to change your mind and obey Our orders so that we might mutually keep the peace?[25]

The tone was highly displeasing to the Japanese, but Kanenaga, hard-pressed and perhaps hoping for China's help in his losing fight, responded favorably. Even after the Chinese discovered that Kanenaga was not the king of Japan, they continued to address him as such until 1386 when Hung-wu broke relations with Japan. The initiative for reestablishing relations later came from Japan.

By 1396 Yoshimitsu had destroyed most of the last remnants of Southern Court resistance and had established himself as the master of all Japan. He now was able to turn his eyes abroad, and in the following year, in the hopes of establishing trade and cultural relations with China, he sent a first embassy.[26] Four years later, in 1401, Yoshimitsu sent a second embassy, this one with a message couched in deferential terms asking for the renewal of the friendly relations between Japan and China that had existed ever since Japan was founded. Gifts were sent, and although they were not designated as tribute, that surely was how the Chinese interpreted them. The gifts included a thousand taels in gold, swords, horses, fans, and armor.

Two Chinese ambassadors returned the visit, in 1402 reaching Hyōgo, where they were met by Yoshimitsu himself. The Chinese ambassadors, appreciating Yoshimitsu's deferential language, replied with genial flattery. The emperor's rescript, also couched in friendly terms, included the words: "Japan has always been called a country of poems and books, and it has always been in Our heart."[27] From then on, the exchange of embassies became routine.

The Chinese government agreed to allow one tribute-bearing ship from Japan every ten years. But this restriction was generally ignored, and ships often traveled between the two countries. Articles imported from China included works of art, religious and literary books, and what were known as *karamono* (Chinese things), the unusual and precious wares of a country whose civilization had reached a far higher stage of development than Japan's, as Yoshimitsu recognized.

In the hopes of being richly rewarded by the Chinese court, Yoshimitsu agreed to destroy the Japanese pirates who had been plundering the Chinese coast. He carried out this promise with severity. As George Sansom related, "According to a credible account, one of the first missions under the new trade agreement presented a number of captives to the Emperor of China. His Majesty politely returned them to the Japanese leaders, who had them boiled alive."[28]

In 1403 Yoshimitsu accepted from the Chinese emperor the title of King of Japan. The imperial rescript sent by Emperor Chien-wen stated in part, "You, Minamoto Dōgi,[29] King of Japan, with a heart ever with the Imperial Household and holding true to your love of your ruler, have sent envoys to come to the Court, crossing over the waves and billows."[30] The rescript, though friendly in tone, revealed that no less than Hung-wu, Chien-wen considered himself to be the overlord of Japan. According to Chinese accounts, Yoshimitsu was given a crown and robes of state, confirming his status as a lesser monarch and a loyal ally of the Middle Kingdom. In later times, as we have seen, his willingness to accept the title of king from the Chinese court would arouse the fierce indignation of Japanese patriots.

In his role as a vassal of the Chinese emperor, Yoshimitsu offered tribute of swords, fans, and works of artisan craftsmanship and received in return far more valuable gifts—silver, jade, silks, brocades, pearls, and the like. The Chinese stipulation that tribute missions visit their country only once in ten years seems to have been inspired by the imbalance between the simple offerings made by tributary countries and the lavish gifts that the Chinese, as the suzerain state, felt obliged to provide. The Japanese were struck dumb with amazement when they saw the splendor of the first shipment of Chinese gifts.[31]

Yoshimitsu was happy to refer to himself as the king of Japan in the letters he sent to the Chinese court.[32] Although he behaved as a despot in Japan, his letters to China were obsequious. Entranced with China, he wore Chinese clothes at court, and before reading messages received from the Chinese court, he would always light incense in reverence. Yoshimitsu behaved like a vassal of the Middle Kingdom not only in the language he used in documents sent to the Chinese court but also in the privacy of his palace.

Yoshimitsu's successor, Yoshimochi, was far less worshipful of China. In 1411 he refused to receive a Chinese envoy who brought a letter and a gift of money from Emperor Yung-lo. According to Sansom, "His own explanation was that Yoshimitsu, after being attacked by the disease which was to prove fatal, had vowed never again to offend the national deities by receiving envoys from a foreign country."[33] In 1418 Yung-lo sent Yoshimochi another letter, politely but firmly reproving him for not behaving properly as a vassal and warning that the Chinese army and navy were far stronger than those of the Mongols, whose attacks on Japan had been repulsed 150 years earlier. In reply, Yoshimochi declared that he would not receive any further missions from the Chinese court. Official intercourse between the two countries, terminated in 1419, was not restored during Yoshimochi's lifetime. A modern Chinese scholar well described the difficulty of establishing and maintaining official relations between Ming China and Japan in terms of the difference in their attitudes with respect to trade:

> For the Japanese, trade was, perhaps, the *raison d'être* for tributary relations otherwise undesirable and humiliating. For the Chinese government, trade was an annoying aspect of the system, to be limited as much as possible. It regarded the periodic Japanese missions as primarily of a symbolic tributary character and was anxious to restrict the numbers of members of Japanese embassies, as well as the quantities of merchandise they brought with them to China.[34]

Relations with China were renewed by Yoshimochi's successor, Yoshinori. In 1432 the Chinese emperor Hsüan-te sent a rescript to Yoshinori through the king of Ryūkyū urging the new shogun to follow the example of Yoshimitsu and promising to treat the Japanese generously. Yoshinori responded favorably, sending a priest of the Tenryū-ji as his ambassador.

Japan gradually came to depend on China for such essentials of modern life as coins. Most of the coins in circulation were Eiraku-sen, so called because they had been struck during the reign of Emperor Yung-lo (1403–1424), pronounced Eiraku in Japan. In

1464, for example, Yoshimasa sent an envoy to the Ming court asking for copper coins, reminding the Chinese that in the Yung-lo era the Japanese had received a great quantity of these coins. The coins had since become scarce, causing economic hardship because the expansion of internal trade in Japan had increased the need for currency beyond the country's capacity to mint coins.

The fact that the coins bore the name of a foreign ruler did not bother the Japanese. Although they did not adopt the Chinese calendar or take Chinese-style names, as the Koreans did, they were profoundly indebted to the Great Ming dynasty, and this was a source of pride and not of shame.

The situation did not change during Yoshimasa's reign. In 1453, when a Japanese envoy left for China, he took with him a memorial from Yoshimasa that said in part, "I, your subject, Minamoto Yoshinari, following respectfully the will of my forefathers, have succeeded to the rulership of this poor country. I am preserving this distant land for the sole purpose of being your outer defenses. On account of many internal troubles, I have delayed presenting tribute."[35]

Yoshimasa, no less than his grandfather, was ready to identify himself as a vassal of the Great Ming. Paradoxically, the Higashiyama era—broadly speaking, the fifty or so years between Yoshimasa's accession to the post of shogun and his death in 1490[36]—was marked by a steady Japanization of cultural forms borrowed from China and the emergence of a distinctively Japanese aesthetic that persists to this day.

5

One of Ashikaga Yoshimasa's worst defects, at least
in the eyes of his detractors, was his unbridled passion for building costly palaces. His first domicile
after he became shogun in 1443 was the Karasumaru
Palace, originally the home of his mother's cousin
Karasumaru Suketō. Not having been constructed
as a shogun's residence, the palace lacked adequate
rooms for receiving visitors or for conducting other
state functions, and the original building had to be
enlarged for the shogun's use, with adjoining pavilions that included a private study and a chapel where
he might worship. Some additions were cannibal-
ized from earlier palaces, and others were newly
constructed. Yoshimasa lived for sixteen years in the
Karasumaru Palace. This was where he received his

education, and it probably had nostalgic associations, but as he grew older he became dissatisfied with the outmoded buildings.

At first Yoshimasa planned nothing more ambitious than a remodeling of the Karasumaru Palace. Extensive renovations were in fact made, but hardly had they been completed in 1458 than Yoshimasa decided, to the astonishment of his court, to move the buildings of the renovated Karasumaru Palace to the site of the old Muromachi Palace, familiarly known as Hana no gosho (Palace of Flowers).[1]

The first Palace of Flowers had been erected on the site in 1368 as the residence of Retired Emperor Sūkō. The original building was destroyed in 1377 in a conflagration, but in 1431 Ashikaga Yoshinori built a new Palace of Flowers on the site. Parts of Yoshinori's palace were used when the Karasumaru Palace was moved to Muromachi in 1458. Criticism of Yoshimasa's extravagance in renovating a palace only to move it elsewhere, despite the huge costs, was privately expressed in diaries of the time, though naturally no one openly expressed opposition.[2]

It is not clear why Yoshimasa felt he needed to change the location of the Karasumaru Palace. Morita Kyōji, the author of a study of Yoshimasa, wrote,

Yoshimasa had his own special aesthetic sense with respect to the culture in which he lived. The locus where his aesthetic sense was given substance was invariably the palace where he resided. The embodiment of the aesthetic sensibility he displayed in the Palace of Flowers would be continued and further developed in the Higashiyama mountain retreat where he lived after his retirement.[3]

Perhaps Yoshimasa, believing that the Karasumaru Palace was in the taste of an earlier generation, wanted a building that would more faithfully reflect his taste. If this was in fact his attitude, it was rather unusual. When constructing new buildings, Japanese rulers were more likely to make a point of following precedents than to insist on their own preferences. It was unlikely that Yoshimasa, who all but worshiped Yoshimitsu, was consciously rebelling against his grandfather's tastes, but perhaps without fully realizing it, he had, by the age of twenty-two, developed tastes of his own that required expression.

Construction began immediately on the new Palace of Flowers, at first using elements from the dismantled Karasumaru Palace. The ridgepole of the *kaisho* (reception hall) was erected in the second month of 1459, and other buildings were quickly added. In the eleventh month of that year, Yoshimasa moved into the new palace.

Contemporary diarists described in terms of wonderment the magnificence of the buildings and gardens.[4] Although these accounts contain numerous exclamations of admiration for the surpassing skill displayed in the new palace, the details are not concrete enough for us to form a clear picture of what made the appearance of the palace seem so remarkable, but it is likely that it reflected in some way Yoshimasa's fondness for things in the Chinese taste. For example, Unsen Taikyoku used the phrase "rare plants and curious rocks" (*kika chinseki*) when praising the garden, an indication that it probably was in Chinese, rather than traditional Japanese, taste.

A difference between the aesthetic ideals of the two countries was indirectly suggested by the priest Kenkō in *Tsurezuregusa* (*Essays in Idleness*) when, after describing the flowers that he thought desirable in a gentleman's garden, he added: "It is hard to feel affection for other plants—those rarely encountered, or which have unpleasant-sounding Chinese names, or which look peculiar. As a rule, oddities and rarities are enjoyed by persons of no breeding. It is best to be without them."[5] Kenkō preferred ordinary flowers to exotic plants and did not share Yoshimasa's taste for "rare plants and curious rocks," even though they were essential to Chinese gardens.

In 1462 Yoshimasa built the luxurious Takakura Palace for his mother, Hino Shigeko. This palace and its magnificent garden were constructed at a time when the city of Kyoto was still suffering the effects of the famine in which more than eighty thousand people died. In addition to the extravagance of building these palaces, Yoshimasa repeatedly staged elaborate and very costly parties, notably a cherry-blossom viewing in 1465.

Although many buildings were destroyed during the Ōnin War, the new Palace of Flowers miraculously survived the destruction and looting of the first (and worst) years, only to burn to the ground in 1476. Fires set in pawnshops and saké shops by rioters who had been angered by profiteering spread to the houses of the nobles and eventually to the Palace of Flowers, where the treasures of generations of shoguns went up in smoke.[6] Yoshimasa, driven from the palace by the flames, took refuge along with his wife and his son Yoshihisa in the Kokawa Palace, a villa belonging to Hosokawa Katsumoto.

Three years earlier, in 1473, Yoshimasa had resigned from the post of shogun in favor of Yoshihisa. Affairs of state, however, remained in Yoshimasa's hands because the new shogun was only eight years old. Yoshihisa did not stay long at the Kokawa Palace but soon moved to the house of Ise Sadamune (the heir of Sadachika), apparently after a quarrel with Yoshimasa. The precocious Yoshihisa seems to have resented his father's refusal to yield the privileges of the office of shogun to his eleven-year-old son. As if to demonstrate that he was quite capable of performing the duties of a shogun, Yoshihisa threw himself into studying the poetry of the Heian era, and after 1480, poem competitions (*utakai*), carried out in strict obedience to the traditions of four hundred years earlier, were held in his presence. Courtiers who favored the cause of the young shogun eagerly participated in these contests.

In these and other studies, Yoshihisa had the benefit of the advice of Ichijō Kaneyoshi, the most distinguished scholar of the day. Kaneyoshi stressed the importance of maintaining the old court traditions. Under his influence, the shogun's court announced plans for compiling a new, imperially sponsored collection of *waka* poetry. The last such collection, the twenty-first, had been compiled by Kaneyoshi in 1439. The plan for a new anthology, postponed by the war, finally was abandoned with the death of Kaneyoshi in 1481.

In 1480 Kaneyoshi presented to Yoshihisa "Shōdan chiyō" (A Woodcutter's Talks on Good Government), intended as an introduction to politics for the young shogun. He offered his opinions on such specific matters as the extreme care that the shogun must take when appointing military governors and personal attendants, as well as more general advice on the principles of good government. With respect to religion, Kaneyoshi believed that the old Buddhism (the Nara sects, Tendai, and Shingon) was too complicated for contemporary people to understand. He advised Yoshihisa instead to combine the best parts of two more recent sects, Zen and Jōdo (Pure Land) Buddhism. Although the tenets of the two sects were in many ways antithetical, he believed there was much to be learned from both.[7]

Kaneyoshi's advice on literary, political, and religious matters probably was beneficial to Yoshihisa, but the young man was highly strung and given to displays of temper. Relations between him and his father, and especially between the partisans of each, became increasingly hostile.[8] Yoshihisa more than once threatened to shave his head and "leave the world" as a sign of frustration over the awkward position of being the shogun but enjoying none of the privileges. On one occasion, he cut his topknot and planned to run away, but he was restrained by Ise Sadamune and by the personal letter that Yoshimasa sent him, urging Yoshihisa to abandon his plan.[9]

In 1480 Yoshihisa took as his consort a daughter of Hino Yoshikatsu. Even during the early days of his marriage, however, he continued his affair with a woman who was a particular favorite of Yoshimasa's, adding sexual rivalry to their political disputes.[10]

In the spring of 1481, Yoshimasa quarreled with his wife, Tomiko. This was not their first serious quarrel: in 1471 Tomiko had left the Muromachi Palace and gone to live with her mother. For a time, husband and wife lived apart, and after an even more violent altercation in 1481, the separation became permanent. Yoshimasa, now cut off from both wife and son by quarrels, may have felt a sense of liberation. He was free to do as he pleased.

One rainy night,[11] Yoshimasa secretly left the Kokawa Palace, accompanied by four or five retainers, and made his way to his mountain retreat in Iwakura, north of the capital. Emperor Go-Tsuchimikado was shocked to learn that Yoshimasa was not in the Kokawa Palace. Although he ordered him to return to the capital, Yoshimasa, paying no attention to the emperor's command, began to make arrangements for having his head shaved and becoming a priest.[12]

Various reasons have been suggested for his decision to "leave the world" at this particular time. He had been upset ever since the Ōnin War because the military governors had ceased to pay attention to his orders. The quarrels with Tomiko and Yoshihisa had also contributed to his disenchantment with the world. He was particularly aggrieved because Yoshihisa, whom he had urged to take care of his health (meaning that he disapproved of the dissolute life Yoshihisa was leading), had ostentatiously ignored his advice. Although Yoshihisa was still only sixteen, he had become a profligate. But regardless of the reasons for taking the step at this time, Yoshimasa had for years wanted to become a monk and was looking forward to spending his declining years (he was now forty-five years old) in quiet retirement.

As far back as 1466, Yoshimasa had chosen Higashiyama, a section of the capital known for its beautiful scenery, as the site of his future retreat. He made detailed plans for the residence, using for reference the architectural drawings of one of the Konoe palaces. Arrangements were made for obtaining the necessary construction workers and building materials; but with the outbreak of the Ōnin War, Yoshimasa was deprived of much of his income, making it impossible for him to build a retreat with his usual extravagance.

Although thwarted in carrying out his plans by the war, Yoshimasa did not forget them. His move to Iwakura from the Kokawa Palace may have been planned as a intermediate stage to his final destination, the retreat in the Higashiyama hills. The land he chose belonged to the Jōdo-ji, a Tendai temple that had been founded in the Heian period but was destroyed during the Ōnin War. Ashikaga Yoshimi (known at that time as Gijin) had served as the abbot of the temple before Yoshimasa persuaded him to return to the laity.

The picturesque site of the retreat contrasted with the urban location of Yoshimasa's earlier dwellings. Following the Chinese usage, the Japanese gave temples "mountain names" and referred to them as if they were situated on a mountainside even if they stood on flat ground in the middle of Kyoto. Yoshimasa wanted to live on a more authentic mountain, but unlike a true hermit, he sought a retreat not in the wilderness but in a place of quiet scenic beauty, not too far from the city.

Construction of the retreat was begun on the fourth day of the second month (February 21) of 1482. On the twenty-fifth of the month, Yoshimasa, taking advantage of a supposed *katatagae* (forbidden direction), went to inspect the preliminary construction.[13] To pay the building costs, he had imposed levies on the military governors of various provinces, but most, aware of the shogun's inability to enforce his orders, failed to respond. There were some exceptions among the daimyos, and a few rich families gave money, but there was not enough to cover the expenses generated by Yoshimasa's extravagant tastes.

Yoshimasa must surely have been aware of the difficulty of raising funds at such a time, so soon after a ten-year war, but he intended to make his retreat incorporate his aesthetic conceptions as closely as possible. When military governors refused funds and workmen, Yoshimasa turned to temples, shrines, and other institutions that were normally exempt from taxation, especially to those in the region immediately surrounding the capital, the last remaining stronghold of the shogunate. Indifferent to the hardships he caused the temples and ultimately the peasants who were condemned to perform long periods of forced labor, Yoshimasa searched for "rare plants and curious rocks" to decorate his retreat.

In the eighth month of 1482, a ceremony was held to commemorate the raising of the central ridgepole of Yoshimasa's future living quarters (*tsunenogosho*) at the Higashiyama retreat. The building was completed in the following year, and Yoshimasa moved in, even though construction work continued all around him. This building would be his home and refuge from the harsh realities of the world for the rest of his life. The day after Yoshimasa took up residence in his new house, Emperor Go-Tsuchimikado bestowed on it the name Higashiyama-dono. Not only the building but also Yoshimasa himself were frequently referred to by this name in documents of the period. (Yoshihisa was similarly known as Muromachi-dono, from the name of the shogunate palace where he lived.)

From this time on, Yoshimasa devoted the greatest attention to the buildings and furnishings of the Higashiyama mountain retreat and its gardens. At least ten separate buildings were planned,[14] but the chronic lack of funds repeatedly delayed their completion. One unusual feature of Yoshimasa's retreat was that unlike the Temple of the Golden Pavilion, where Yoshimitsu had conducted official functions even after entering Buddhist orders, it had no public space; it was meant for the private enjoyment of one man.

After Yoshimasa's death, the retreat was consecrated as a Zen temple and called the Jishō-ji. (The nickname Ginkaku-ji, by which it is popularly known today, dates back to only the Edo period.) The construction was in four stages. The first stage was marked by the building of the *tsunenogosho* in 1483. The second stage, the Saishi-an, the hall of Zen meditation, was completed in the fourth month of 1485. The third stage, the *kaisho*, was completed in the eleventh month of 1487. The fourth stage, the Kannon-den (Ginkaku), was unfinished at the time of Yoshimasa's death in 1490.[15]

The expenses and workmen for these constructions were at first provided by military governors and religious institutions, but contributions from domains outside the home province of Yamashiro ceased altogether after 1485, and Yoshimasa was compelled to beg rich men for financial assistance. His determination to see to completion his grand plan for the Higashiyama retreat no doubt explains his willingness to endure this humiliation. In most matters, he was weak willed and ineffectual; but with respect to the building of the retreat, he was adamant.

Even if we take into account Yoshimasa's determination to achieve perfection in every detail, it may seem odd that it should have taken more than eight years to complete a small number of relatively simple structures. The slowness of the completion of the planned buildings was occasioned mainly by the irregularity with which gifts of money and workmen were received; but perhaps completion was most often delayed by Yoshimasa himself, who, when dissatisfied with some feature of a structure, would insist that it be modified or even totally rebuilt.

Europeans who visited the Ginkaku-ji in the nineteenth century were generally unimpressed by the little buildings in the garden, perhaps because they unconsciously compared this retreat of a shogun with the palaces of the kings of Europe. The Ginkaku-ji is certainly no Versailles, nor does it resemble in the slightest the Escorial, the mausoleum that Philip II of Spain built to preserve his glory. Although he devoted the last years of his life to building the Ginkaku-ji, Yoshimasa seems not to have been impelled by the desire to immortalize himself. Palaces he had built were destroyed by fire even in times of peace, and he knew from the experience of the Ōnin War how unlikely it was that any building could long resist destruction. Indeed, he may actually have courted it. For all his admiration of China, it did not occur to Yoshimasa (or anyone else of that time) to build in brick or stone in the manner of Chinese temples. Instead, Yoshimasa chose to follow Japanese tradition and used only the most perishable materials—wood and paper—as if to demonstrate his awareness of perishability as an essential element in beauty. His testament to the world—the Higashiyama retreat—is indeed a thing of beauty, but he probably did not expect it to defy the ravages of time. Paradoxically, it has lasted longer than many supposedly deathless monuments.

On July 26, 1485, Yoshimasa entered Buddhist orders at a sub-temple of the Rinzai-ji in Saga, northwest of the capital. He had long wished to follow Ashikaga Yoshimitsu in shaving his head as a sign that he had withdrawn from worldly concerns. In Yoshimitsu's case, entering Buddhist orders was a means of establishing himself as the power behind the throne, rather like the cloistered emperors of the late Heian period who, despite their Buddhist robes, still controlled affairs of state. By this time, however, Yoshimasa had lost all ambitions for this world and desired only the freedom to enjoy spiritual pleasures without being hampered by state duties. Some believe that he took the step quite suddenly, exasperated over the quarrels between his followers and those who supported his son, the shogun.[16] But he was in fact carrying out a plan he had conceived two years earlier. At that time, he was stopped from shaving his head by Emperor Go-Tsuchimikado, but now he was not to be prevented from his resolution.

Yoshimasa was inducted as a priest of the Rinzai branch of Zen. He chose Ōsen Keisan (1429–1493), a monk known more for the excellence of his Chinese poetry than for his piety, to administer the tonsure. Yoshimasa took the Buddhist name Dōkei, recalling Yoshimitsu's Buddhist name, Dōgi. Although he was now officially a priest, his new status did not bring about any marked change in his behavior. He probably did not spend much time reading texts of Zen. In 1464 he had attended fifteen sessions of lectures on *Rinzairoku* but frankly confessed afterward that he could make no sense of what he had heard.[17] Nothing indicates that he regularly practiced sitting in Zen meditation.

The influence of Zen, though of immense importance to Yoshimasa both culturally and artistically, seems not to have greatly affected his personal religion. For comfort in an age of warfare and political uncertainty, Yoshimasa, like many in high places, turned to Amida Buddha, who had vowed to save all who called on him. Haga Kōshirō suggested that Yoshimasa's belief in Jōdo Buddhism may have been transmitted from the imperial family.

The diary of Sanjōnishi Sanetaka (1455–1537) plainly states that all three emperors who reigned during the Higashiyama era were devout believers in Jōdo Buddhism, even though the imperial family had traditionally been closely connected with Tendai Buddhism. Jōdo priests were frequently summoned to the palace to deliver sermons to the emperor, members of the court, and court ladies. The *nenbutsu*, the invocation of Amida Buddha's name as a prayer for salvation, was widely practiced. Abbot Jinson of the Daijō-in (1430–1508), the son of Ichijō Kaneyoshi, recorded in his diary during the third month of 1478 that "everybody in the imperial palace says the *nenbutsu*."[18]

Although the Jishō-ji became a Zen temple after Yoshimasa's death and the general plan of the buildings was borrowed from another Zen temple, the Saihō-ji, the name of its chief hall revealed Yoshimasa's Jōdo leanings. When he asked his advisers to decide on a name for the hall where his personal Buddha (*jibutsu*) was to be enshrined, he directed them to choose one that was connected in some way with the name of a similar hall at the Saihō-ji but would indicate that an Amida triptych was enshrined within. The name they selected was Tōgu-dō. The characters mean literally "east seek hall," but the expanded meaning was apparently "a person in the East seeks the Pure Land in the West."[19] The *fusuma* paintings in the hall that enshrined Yoshimasa's personal Buddha were the work of Kanō Masanobu. The paintings were of the Ten Monks described by Shan-tao (613–681), the first to teach the central importance of saying the *nenbutsu*. Volumes of the Jōdo text *Ōjō yōshū* (*Essentials of Salvation*) lay on a desk in the room, and in front of the Tōgu-dō a lotus pond had been created, alluding to the belief that those saved by Amida Buddha would be reborn on lotuses in the Pure Land. The Zen priest Kisen Shūshō (1424–1493), who visited Yoshimasa in 1487, wrote in his diary, "The place truly deserves to be called the Paradise in the West."[20]

Jōdo Buddhism supplied Yoshimasa with religious comfort, assuring him that when he left this world of dust and evil he would be reborn in Amida's paradise, but his aesthetic preferences were most deeply affected by Zen. At this time, Zen priests dominated the intellectual life. Learning was preserved in the Zen monasteries rather as it had been in the monasteries of medieval Europe. A knowledge of classical Chinese was indispensable to any monk in order to read the sacred texts of Buddhism, but the Zen monks of this time were far more than merely literate. Their poetry and prose in Chinese included works of considerable literary distinction.

These writings are known today as *Gozan bungaku* (*Literature of the Five Mountains*) because monks at five great temples ("mountains")—Nanzen-ji, Tenryū-ji, Shōkoku-ji, Kennin-ji, and Tōfuku-ji—were of predominant importance in creating this new literature. The monks led privileged lives. Even during periods of warfare and other disasters, the patronage of shoguns, military governors, and the high-ranking nobility shielded the monks of the Five Mountains from the hardships that people elsewhere suffered. Lesser Zen temples that did not have such generous patrons might experience economic hardship, but their priests probably had the satisfaction of telling themselves that they, unlike the priests of the

Five Mountains, lived in faithful obedience to the orthodox Zen prescription of "honest poverty."

The priests of the Five Mountains led lives that differed very little from those of the laity. We know from their diaries that they enjoyed gatherings at which they composed Chinese poems, attended drinking parties more often than lectures on religious and secular works, and indulged in gossip about politics and other priests. The diaries almost never mention sitting in Zen meditation or performing Buddhist rites. Some Zen monks of strong religious convictions deplored the worldly atmosphere of the great monasteries, none more so than Ikkyū Sōjun, who, disgusted with the worldly activities of the priests at the Daitoku-ji, flagrantly disregarded the rules of priestly conduct and gave himself openly to sensual pleasure, in this way expressing his contempt for the hypocritical behavior of seemingly pious priests.

In 1440, when services were held at the Daitoku-ji, the temple to which Ikkyū was long attached, on the thirteenth anniversary of the death of Ikkyū's master, Kasō Sōdon, parishioners had assembled, bearing lavish gifts for the occasion. Ikkyū was annoyed by what he took for unseemly commotion at a ceremony honoring his master, and the lavish gifts seemed to him a profanation of Zen. He therefore decided to sever relations with the temple, but before he left he composed a poem addressed to Yōsō Sōi, the abbot of the Daitoku-ji, whom Ikkyū had elsewhere denounced as a poisonous snake, a seducer, and a leper. The poem ran:

> For ten days in the temple my mind's been in turmoil.
> My feet are entangled in endless red strings.
> If some day you get around to looking for me,
> Try the fish shop, the wine parlor, or the brothel.

Angered by ten days of vulgar commercial activities in the temple, Ikkyū defiantly announced that he was fleeing the temple for the sanctity of the fish shop (though priests were forbidden to eat fish), the wine parlor (though drinking liquor was also forbidden), or (most shockingly) the brothel.[21]

The disgust aroused in Ikkyū by the mundane lives led by the priests at the Daitoku-ji was understandable given the ideals of Zen. It might be argued, however, that it was precisely because luxury-loving monks violated the austere ideals of earlier Zen masters that their contributions to Japanese culture were so extensive. For example, the monks of Ikkyū's time generally obeyed the Buddhist commandment against eating meat or fish, but instead of restricting themselves to a simple meal of one soup and one vegetable, as had the Zen monks of earlier times, the monks of the Five Mountains varied their diet with delicacies originally imported from China, including noodles, tofu, and *nattō* (fermented beans). At first these vegetarian foods were eaten only in the Zen monasteries, but gradually they spread to the entire country and even came to be considered particularly typical of the Japanese diet. Japanese cuisine, too, had its inception in the Higashiyama era.[22]

Even if Zen—whether because of the difficulty of its texts or its insistence on achieving salvation through one's own efforts—was not suited to Yoshimasa, who was neither philosophical by disposition nor inclined to devote himself assiduously to religious ideals, it provided a congenial background for the intellectual and aesthetic life he wished to pursue. His manner of life did not change much as a result of entering orders. It is true that sometimes (as we know from surviving accounts) he ate extremely simple food, but this was probably less because of religious conviction than because he had grown tired of his normally elaborate meals. He seems, however, to have regretted the dissolute life he had earlier led, as a poem suggests. It bears the headnote, "Living a quiet life in the Tōgu-dō, on the night of the fifteenth of the eighth month, visitors came and I wrote this poem":

kuyashiku zo	Today I recall
sugishi uki yo wo	The sad world where I lived
kyō zo omou	With bitter regret—
kokoro kumanaki	My mind serene as I gaze
tsuki wo nagamete	At a moon free of shadows.[23]

The poem suggests not merely regret over time wasted in meaningless pleasures but also the purification that Yoshimasa now felt emanating from the clarity of the moon, a familiar Buddhist symbol of enlightenment. Another poem was interpreted by Haga Kōshirō as meaning that Yoshimasa had moved to a higher stage of aesthetic appreciation from his earlier preference for positive, rich beauty to an awareness of negative, incomplete beauty:

wa ga io wa	My little hut stands
tsukimachiyama no	At the foot of the mountain
fumoto nite	"Waiting for the Moon"
katamuku tsuki no	And my thoughts go to the light
kage wo shi zo omou	Of the moon sinking in the sky.[24]

It is possible to detect in this poem and others composed at the Higashiyama retreat the first expression of Yoshimasa's appreciation of the quiet, subdued, refined beauty associated with the term *wabi*. The Ginkaku-ji would be the embodiment of this new interest.

6

Up until the time that Ashikaga Yoshimasa took up residence at the Ginkaku-ji, he had contributed almost nothing to the welfare of the Japanese people of his time or to the culture of future generations. He had been a total failure as shogun: although he bore the title of "barbarian-subduing great general," he had subdued neither barbarians nor civilized men. He had never commanded an army in the field or negotiated an alliance that might have strengthened the shogunate, which had grown progressively weaker until, toward the end of his reign, the military governors could ignore its wishes with impunity.

Some recent scholars have praised Yoshimasa's good sense in refusing to get involved in the senseless Ōnin War. This was, at best, a negative merit. His

refusal to head the shogunate forces during the war was not a decision reached after agonizing over his proper course of action but
a passive recognition of his impotence as a leader at a time when
resolute action was needed. In his own day and ever since, Yoshimasa has ranked as one of the least effective shoguns in all of
Japanese history.

Yoshimasa was no more successful in his private life. His many
early involvements with women (including Imamairi, his mistress
or surrogate mother, put to death perhaps by his order) brought
him no lasting joy, and his married life was a disaster. Accounts of
the period, beginning with *Ōnin ki*, depict him as a man so lacking
a will of his own that he was no more than a helpless tool in the
hands of his fearsome wife, Hino Tomiko. Perhaps such accounts
are exaggerated and Yoshimasa was actually not so completely
under Tomiko's dominance, but this was how he appeared to the
world. He could not control her least attractive feature, her craving for money, and this may have been why he eventually broke
with her and the two lived apart. His relations with his son Yoshihisa were equally unsatisfactory, though the causes of their mutual
hostility can only be conjectured. By the time the Ōnin War ended,
Yoshimasa probably seemed a failure even to himself, in both his
public and his private life.

However, if we turn our attention to the latter part of Yoshimasa's life, especially to his activities after he went to live at the
mountain retreat he built in the Higashiyama area of Kyoto, our
impressions of the man are likely to be quite different. The
Higashiyama era was one of the most brilliant periods of Japanese
cultural history, and the guiding spirit was the same Yoshimasa who
had been a failure in everything else he did. Of course, not every
cultural development of the Higashiyama era can be credited to
this one man, but Yoshimasa's taste was reflected in many of the
distinctive artistic developments of the time. His cultural legacy to
the Japanese people has been immense.

Only two buildings of Yoshimasa's retreat survive. Perhaps their most unexpected feature is that the interiors do not surprise us or give us the feeling that a great lapse of time separates Yoshimasa's world from our own. Far from it—the rooms look very familiar, so like those in countless other Japanese buildings we have seen that it is easy to forget that they are half a thousand years old.

We would not have the same feeling if, by means of a time machine, we were able to step into a room of a Heian palace. It would certainly look unfamiliar, though we would be aware that the building was Japanese. We might recognize certain features even without any special knowledge of Heian architecture, if only because similar rooms are depicted in the magnificent horizontal scrolls illustrating *The Tale of Genji* and other classics of Heian literature. Murasaki Shikibu so magically evoked the characters that we may feel we know and understand them, but they lived in buildings that belonged to another world.

Perhaps the most striking feature of the lives of the Heian aristocrats she describes was the manner of courtship. We learn from the novel, for example, that Genji might never have had so much as a glimpse of a woman with whom he thought he was in love and to whom he sent poems expressing the depth of his feelings. It is hard for us to imagine a man's passion being inflamed by a woman's handwriting or by a glimpse of her sleeves, all that was visible as she sat inside her *kichō* ("screen of state," in Arthur Waley's translation). Indeed, he might not actually see his lady friend until they had became lovers and perhaps not even then. The *kichō*—the elaborate curtains that protected women from the eyes of male visitors—were probably the feature of a Heian palace room that would most surprise us.

We know also from Heian paintings that bright green tatami mats covered only a small part of the floor. (It was not until the Higashiyama era that tatami covered the entire floor.) A Heian room contained almost no immovable furniture: there was no cupboard in which to store kimonos that were not in use, no case in which to put books, no wall space on which to display objects of art, no desk on which to write a letter, no table from which to eat a meal. The rooms probably were not only uncomfortable but also dark. Shutters known as *hajitomi* let in some light, but because they also had the function of protecting court ladies from the gaze of people outside, the shutters contributed to the darkness of a room rather than illuminating it.

Shōji, like those used in modern Japan, which admit light through translucent paper, had not yet been invented in Heian Japan,[1] but they are found in the Dōjinsai,[2] the tea room of the Tōgu-dō, one of the Ginkaku-ji's two surviving buildings. The *shōji*, intended originally to admit light to the desk in one corner of the room, became an indispensable feature of later Japanese architecture. They help account for the familiarity we feel on entering the Dōjinsai, and they make us forget how much else has changed in Japan since Yoshimasa's day.

The Dōjinsai, four and a half tatami in size, resembles innumerable similar rooms in temples and private houses all over Japan for the simple reason that it was their model. Every Japanese-style building constructed since the sixteenth century owes something to the architecture here. The *shōji*, the *chigaidana* (staggered shelves), the layout of the tatami in the tea room, the ceiling, the square interior pillars, the desk, and the space provided for the display of flowers or objects of art all are characteristic of the *shoin-zukuri* architecture, which reached definitive expression in Yoshimasa's retreat. Almost any Japanese, even if he lives by choice in a reinforced-concrete apartment house, is likely to feel a sense of "coming home" when he enters the Dōjinsai. This architecture is a part of the living culture of Japan; by contrast, a Heian room is a distant ancestor.

It is not only the interiors of the buildings at the Ginkaku-ji that seem familiar and peculiarly Japanese. The gardens (both green and sand), the ponds, the trees, and the surrounding scenery all contribute to a feeling of a total immersion in nature, the ideal of countless Japanese over the centuries. Here Yoshimasa watched the four seasons as they came and went, and he was constantly aware of the birds and insects that each season brought. We, too, can share in his pleasures, and we are likely to feel that we are in a truly Japanese place.

Love of the moon and of nature in general is well attested in Japanese literature from a very early period and deserves its place as a central part of the "soul of Japan." It also is part of the "soul of England," as anyone knows who has visited the gardens of England or read English poetry. But if one is looking for a specifically Japanese example of this phenomenon, I wonder whether the best place to find it is not Yoshimasa's mountain retreat.

Much of the tangible culture of the Muromachi period has disappeared. The Ōnin War and the battles of the sixteenth century destroyed most of the temples, palaces, and other buildings. Miraculously, two buildings of the Ginkaku-ji escaped the flames, though the others were destroyed during the warfare of 1548. The surviving buildings—the Ginkaku and the Tōgu-dō—have been restored on several occasions, and certain features altered, but they are essentially unchanged, and standing inside the Dōjinsai, it is not difficult to imagine a tea ceremony presided over by Yoshimasa.

It might even be possible to assemble bowls, *chashaku* (tea ladles), *mizusashi* (jugs), and other utensils of the tea ceremony that Yoshimasa had personally used, but this is not necessary; the scene does not require priceless antiques to be convincing. There is no need, either, for the Chinese paintings with which Yoshimasa decorated his retreat, though some of them have also survived the perils of the centuries. What is essential is the atmosphere engendered by the tea room. If we were enabled by a time machine to attend a *chanoyu* gathering of Yoshimasa's time, probably little would surprise us because the traditions have remained unbroken.

The first structures to be completed in 1482 at the Higashiyama retreat were the gate and the kitchen, followed in the ninth month of 1483 by the *tsunenogosho*, or living quarters.[3] Yoshimasa moved to this building as soon as it was ready. He seems to have been eager to shake off his past life as quickly as possible.

Yoshimasa probably had long considered exactly how he wished to have his retreat decorated. Hardly had the first building been erected than Kanō Masanobu set about painting on the *fusuma* the *Eight Views of the Hsiao and Hsiang Rivers*. Although Masanobu, the founder of the Kanō school of painting, had never visited China and therefore had no personal knowledge of the celebrated scenery along the two rivers, he was familiar with their features from Chinese paintings of the subject, and inspired by old models, he painted his conception of what the rivers were like. When he had finished the set of paintings, they were embellished by poems in Chinese describing the scenery, composed by monks.

Yoshimasa was evidently pleased with Masanobu's paintings. When the Saishi-an, the hall for Zen meditation, was built in 1485, Masanobu was asked to paint the *fusuma*, and later the same year he was commanded to paint the *fusuma* at the Tōgu-dō. This hall was erected in keeping with the other half of Yoshimasa's Buddhist beliefs, his worship of Amida Buddha. A statue of Amida was the central divinity (*honzon*) of the Tōgu-dō. At Yoshimasa's command, as we have seen, Masanobu painted the Ten Monks on the *fusuma*.[4]

On receiving this commission, Masanobu is reputed to have said to Yoshimasa, "It might seem advisable to do the paintings in the style of the Sung painter Ma Yüan, but in that case, it would be the same as the study in the Saishi-an. I plan to follow the style of Li Lung-mien instead. I'll send you a sample."[5] Yoshimasa asked his art adviser, Sōami, to search in the shogunal storehouse for works by Li Lung-mien that he might inspect before approving Masanobu's plan. However, Sōami was in mourning for his father, and Yoshimasa was unable for some time to examine Li Lung-mien's paintings. He was determined to make sure that paintings in this style met his standards before he gave final approval, even though this delayed the completion of the Tōgu-dō until 1486.

Kanō Masanobu's decision to paint the Ten Monks in the style of Li Lung-mien, rather than of Ma Yüan, the Chinese painter most esteemed in Japan, perhaps stemmed from a desire to display his ability to paint in different styles. He seems not, however, to have considered the possibility of painting in the Yamato-e or some other Japanese style. Masanobu's decision probably reflected Yoshimasa's love of everything Chinese. The Higashiyama era was a time when *karamono*—Chinese things—were prized, imitated, and even worshiped, to the exclusion of specifically Japanese forms of expression.

The love of Chinese art certainly did not begin at this time. Ever since the Nara period, members of the aristocracy had greatly admired and imitated all aspects of Chinese culture, but with Ashikaga Yoshimitsu, this admiration of China developed into uncritical worship. As we have seen, Yoshimitsu was so eager for trade with China that he submitted to the demand of the Chinese court that Japanese wares be labeled as "tribute" from a vassal state to the Middle Kingdom. He accepted this humiliation in part because of the profits that accrued from trade with China but mainly because he was overwhelmed by the beauty of the articles the Chinese emperor bestowed on his vassal, the King of Japan.

Zenrin kokuhō ki, a collection of documents on trade between China and Japan compiled by Zuikei Shūhō (1391–1473), a Zen priest who served both Ashikaga Yoshinori and Yoshimasa, lists the presents bestowed on Yoshinori in 1433 by Emperor Hsüan-tsung. They included three hundred taels in silver, a vast amount of silk fabrics, a palanquin and chairs decorated in red lacquer and gold, silver dishes, saké vessels, brushes, ink, paper, incense wood, tiger and leopard skins, and other rare and exotic treasures. Yoshinori was dazzled by the gifts, and his infatuation with things Chinese was passed on to his son. Yoshimasa ordered from China not only luxuries but also books of Buddhist teachings and Neo-Confucianist philosophy that had yet to reach Japan.

The Zen priests were perhaps even greater worshipers of China than the shoguns. Ever since Zen Buddhism was first introduced to Japan, the models for worship, for the organization of the priesthood, for the architecture of the temples, and for the daily activities of the priests had been obtained from China. The priests initiated trade with China on their own, deriving considerable profits for their temples, but they also served (in their capacity as experts on China) as envoys of the shogunate. They composed the missives that the shoguns sent to China, and when Chinese envoys arrived in Japan, the priests received them. The shogun and the intellectuals of the time turned to Zen priests less for Buddhist enlightenment than for what they might learn from them about Chinese civilization.

The shoguns of the Ashikaga family were aware of being culturally inferior to members of the aristocracy. Although they dutifully studied such avocations of the nobility as the composition of *waka*, the playing of traditional musical instruments, and *kemari* (kickball, the sport favored by the nobles), they probably were resigned to never being able to attain the level of men whose families, from the time of remote ancestors, had been devoted to these accomplishments. The shoguns' enthusiasm for Chinese paintings and antiques thus may have been occasioned by their pleasure in finding an artistic domain in which they could be more expert than the nobles.

The collection of Chinese art formed by Yoshimasa and his immediate predecessors with the guidance of Zen priests was extremely large for that time. A catalogue of the Chinese paintings in the shogunal collection, *Kundaikan sō chōki*, was compiled by Nōami (1397–1471), a "companion" (*dōbōshū*)[6] of the shogun and the keeper of Yoshinori's and Yoshimasa's collection. Theirs was by no means the only notable collection of Chinese paintings in Japan. Zen temples possessed many of the paintings imported from China, especially during the fourteenth century, and others were owned by daimyos; but the shogunate's collection, especially as it developed during the Higashiyama era, was by far the most important. Nōami listed 74 landscape paintings, 91 flower and bird paintings, and 114 Taoist and Buddhist paintings. The painter best represented in the collection was Mu Ch'i, with 103 paintings, followed by Liang K'ai, with 27. All together, some thirty masters of the Sung and Yüan dynasties were represented. But even the 279 paintings that Nōami mentioned were not the shoguns' entire collection; rather, he seems to have confined his catalogue to the masterpieces. The shogun or one of his advisers would periodically go through the collection, weeding out inferior paintings and putting them on sale.

From the beginning, there was the problem of fakes. Once the Chinese learned of the Japanese preference for such artists as Mu Ch'i and Liang K'ai, they happily turned out plausible-looking fakes signed with the names of these artists. Yoshimasa, who had access not only to the shogunal collection but also to the holdings of temples and daimyos, studied the different works attributed to popular artists and eventually became the most accomplished authenticator of Chinese paintings.[7]

The existence of an excellent collection of Chinese paintings was a source of inspiration to Japanese painters. They were fortunate in that Yoshimasa and his predecessors had chosen to acquire works from the finest periods of Chinese painting—the Northern Sung, Southern Sung, and Yüan. The Japanese painters at first devoted themselves to close imitation of the Chinese masterpieces, but gradually they began to assimilate the different Chinese styles and made them their own.

The ink paintings were of particular importance because they created a new variety of Japanese painting. The origin of ink paintings had been a rejection of color, stemming ultimately from Taoist thought.[8] Lao Tzu had said that "the five colors make people blind," meaning that if one's attention is distracted by the colors of things, one will be unable to detect their true forms. A painting in ink, in contrast, was believed to contain all the colors.

The earliest examples of ink painting in Japan were religious. The portraits of Daruma (Bodhidharma) indicate that Zen monks were the first in Japan to experiment with copying Chinese ink paintings as a means of expressing religious beliefs. Being fairly skillful artists, such priests probably did not find it difficult to imitate the techniques of Chinese ink paintings, and the works they produced were competent if not remarkable.

The first truly distinguished priest-painter of the Muromachi period was Josetsu, whose *Catching a Catfish in a Gourd*, painted by command of Ashikaga Yoshimochi, was considered by artists of the Kanō school to be the origin of their art, the earliest successful example in Japan of a distinctive Chinese style of ink painting. A pupil of Josetsu's, Tenshō Shūbun, the official painter (*goyō gaka*) of the shogunate, ruled over the world of Japanese painting in the late fifteenth century. His dates are not known, but he was active during the Higashiyama era and may have painted for Yoshimasa. Very few authenticated paintings by Shūbun survive. Despite his high reputation, the quality of his work has been questioned.[9]

The most famous painter of the Higashiyama era was Sesshū Tōyō (1420–1506). He entered orders as a Zen monk at the Shōkoku-ji while also studying painting with Shūbun. For years he spent much of his time copying Chinese paintings, an experience that probably contributed more to his development as a painter than did his study with Shūbun. In 1467, the year of the outbreak of the Ōnin War, Sesshū, then in his forty-eighth year, traveled to China aboard a ship sent by the shogunate to the Ming court. During his two years in China, he is known to have completed some paintings. One account states that he was chosen to do a painting on a wall of the Ministry of Rites at the imperial palace in Peking.[10] He also made numerous sketches of Chinese landscapes.

Sesshū showed an unusual ability to paint in many different Chinese styles, but he went beyond skillful imitation to achieve a distinctive style of his own. In later years, he recalled his disappointment in the painters he had met in China, a discovery that increased his respect for Josetsu and Shūbun.[11] To show his independence of the Chinese masters, he sometimes signed his paintings Nippon Sesshū, or Sesshū of Japan.

Sesshū returned to Japan in 1469. Kyoto had been devastated by the war and did not seem like a good place for an artist to find work. Yoshimasa, his most likely patron, already had two painters-in-attendance: Kanō Masanobu and Oguri Sōtan (1413–1481). There seemed to be no room for Sesshū in Yoshimasa's service, so he decided to accept the generous patronage of two enlightened daimyo families: the Ōuchi of Suō and the Ōtomo of Bungo. Their patronage enabled him to devote himself to painting without financial worries. He never returned to Kyoto, but in 1483, when Yoshimasa was looking for someone to replace Sōtan (who had died two years earlier), he recalled that Sesshū had been a disciple of Shūbun and asked him to decorate his Higashiyama retreat. Sesshū declined the honor, saying it was not appropriate for a mere priest to paint pictures in a "golden palace." He recommended instead Kanō Masanobu, whose work he particularly admired; he seems not to have been aware that Masanobu was already painting for Yoshimasa.[12] It was generous of Sesshū to propose Masanobu, but one cannot help regretting that Sesshū took no part in decorating the Ginkaku-ji.

Nōami not only compiled a catalogue of the shogunal collection of art but also rated the 156 artists. His omissions are surprising; he included only one Japanese among the artists he discussed: Mokuan Reigen, a Zen priest who had studied in China and died there. Josetsu and Shūbun, both revered by Sesshū, were not mentioned, suggesting that during the Higashiyama era *any* Chinese painting was considered to be better than even the best painting by a Japanese.

One painting of this period stands out in particular, the portrait of the celebrated monk Ikkyū by his disciple Bokusai Shōtō (d. 1492). Unlike more typical paintings of the period, landscapes that are skillful and pleasantly evocative but convey little individuality, Bokusai's portrait of Ikkyū is unforgettable. It is the face of an individual, as striking, strange, and unorthodox as Ikkyū's own life and poetry. At first glance, the portrait may look like a mere sketch from life, its nervous vitality reminiscent of the captured moment of a snapshot, but it was a work of conscious artistry. Ikkyū's growth of beard and unshaven skull, unseemly in a Zen priest, pointed to his great predecessors: Lin-chi (Rinzai), usually depicted unshaven, and in the end Daruma himself, always shown with a beard.[13] The success of the portrait undoubtedly owed much to the subject. This is perhaps the first Japanese portrait that shows a man whose complex character can be read in his face.

Ikkyū, remembered today mainly from children's stories that tell of the irrepressible wit of "Ikkyū-san," was known in his own day for his merciless attacks on corrupt Zen priests. As we have seen, a few of his poems indirectly rebuked Yoshimasa for his extravagance at a time when people were suffering from hunger and the exhaustion brought on by war; but Ikkyū's most savage denunciation was directed against those who (in his opinion) had betrayed the teachings of Zen.

By contrast, the well-known portrait of Yoshimasa, though attributed to Tosa Mitsunobu, an accomplished artist, is disappointing. The background shows a screen painting, suggesting Yoshimasa's fondness for art, but the portrait otherwise tells us almost nothing about the man. The rather stolid face so little resembles the face of the statue of Yoshimasa in the Ginkaku-ji that it seems less a portrait than an effigy intended to convey the dignity of the shogun.

The effigy disappoints because it reveals so little of Yoshimasa's character, whereas the portrait of Ikkyū is unforgettable because it brings out his humanity. Humanity is a quality not often achieved in Muromachi secular painting. In imitation of Chinese examples, human beings are most often no more than decorative elements, tiny figures who serve to bring out the vastness of nature. Such paintings can be highly satisfying, and I myself have sometimes sought refuge in them when exhausted by galleries of sixteenth- or seventeenth-century European depictions of people who all but obliterate the scenery. But how I wish that one of the great European portrait painters (or perhaps Bokusai) had preserved for us the features and character of a man of Yoshimasa's complexity!

7

When Ashikaga Yoshimasa first made his home at the Higashiyama retreat in 1483, the two main buildings were the *tsunenogosho*, his living quarters, and the *kaisho*, the "meeting place." These two buildings have since disappeared, but we know from surviving diaries and other documents not only their external dimensions but how they were divided into rooms with different purposes. We know even which paintings embellished the walls and the *fusuma*. These and the rest of the buildings of the retreat must have constituted one of the loveliest sites in all Japan: buildings, gardens, and superb natural surroundings.

The *tsunenogosho*, the first structure to be completed, was a small building,[1] measuring about forty-two feet north–south and thirty-six feet east–west. These dimensions were not accidental but were modeled on those of the Seiryō Pavilion in the imperial palace.[2]

According to the reconstructed plan of the *tsunenogosho*, Yoshimasa's sleeping place, a six-mat room, was in the very center of the building. Perhaps it was believed that surrounding his bedroom with other rooms would afford protection in case of an attack, but it is surprising that Yoshimasa, who loved gardens, should have agreed to sleep in a room that did not open out onto a garden or another view.

East of the bedroom was an eight-mat room that during the day served as Yoshimasa's office, and to the northeast was a four-mat study. Other rooms were intended variously as a dining room, a room where the *dōbōshū* would await Yoshimasa's commands, and reception rooms for guests. The modesty of the structure indicates that it was designed as a retreat for a man who was weary of worldly pomp.

Yoshimasa encountered many setbacks in carrying out his plans, mainly in finding money, but they did not swerve him from his resolve of building a retreat that exactly accorded with his tastes. He refused to allow modifications made in the interests of economy that might mar the beauty of the retreat. A perfectionist in architecture, no less than in painting, he studied other famous buildings before deciding what would be built at the retreat. While planning the *kaisho*, he paid visits in 1484 and 1485 to the Kinkaku-ji and spent several days there. Even more than the Golden Pavilion itself, he was impressed by the ensemble of temple buildings that met his eyes after climbing to the top of the pavilion.

Yoshimasa's study of the Kinkaku-ji did not tempt him to imitate its splendor. Compared with the Golden Pavilion, the Silver Pavilion would be no more than a shy sibling. Rather, his purpose in visiting the Kinkaku-ji was not to find architectural features to incorporate in the Ginkaku but to immerse himself in the beauty of great architecture. He probably did not hope that his Silver Pavilion would be the equal of the Golden Pavilion but that it would create a feeling of architectural harmony, the most one could hope for in a world that had sadly declined from Yoshimitsu's day.

During the years that Yoshimasa was busily erecting one palace after another inside the city of Kyoto, he had always borne in mind the surroundings of the new buildings and tried to improve them with gardens. There was a limit, however, to what could be done to beautify a site with other buildings nearby. But at Higashiyama he was free to do with the landscape what he chose, and his settings for earlier palaces were dwarfed by the scope of his vision when he set about planning the retreat. It would be flawlessly proportioned, and the buildings would be surrounded by magnificent gardens. Best of all, they would have for their background the lovely Higashiyama hills.

Although he had been ineffectual in performing his duties as shogun, Yoshimasa was resolute in carrying out the plans for his retreat. Having decided, for example, that the gardens must contain imposing trees and ornamental rocks, he commanded that suitable trees and rocks be removed from the gardens of the palaces of Kyoto and brought to Higashiyama. It seems not to have bothered him that the residents of the old palaces might not wish to have their gardens plundered. That was not his only problem. With the primitive means available, a great many laborers were needed to move the heavy trees and rocks from the city to the hills. Luckily for Yoshimasa, in 1488 the daimyo of Echizen offered him three thousand laborers, including a thousand of samurai status, to help dig up, move, and replant at Higashiyama trees that had stood in the garden of the retired emperor's palace.

Construction of the *kaisho*, begun in 1486, was completed in the following year. Funds for erecting the building had been sought throughout the country, but the response was poor. New taxes, said to be temporary, were imposed on the peasants, who were promised that they would be levied on only one occasion, but in fact, they were repeatedly renewed. Whether the tax demands were directed at the peasants or the landowners, they were most often for corvée labor, needed to erect the buildings.[3] In 1485 local samurai (*kokujin*) and peasants, angered by the incessant demands for their labors, rose in a large-scale revolt that was put down only with difficulty.

Yoshimasa officially opened the *kaisho* on November 19, 1487. Three days later, he granted audiences to various nobles who had come to congratulate him on its completion. The *kaisho*, a more impressive building than the *tsunenogosho*,[4] probably stood on the site of the present sand garden of the Ginkaku-ji, surrounded by gardens and looking out over ponds in two directions.

The *kaisho* was an architectural innovation of the Muromachi period. Originally a part of the private house of a member of the aristocracy or the warrior class, it was used mainly for social gatherings. In 1401 Ashikaga Yoshimitsu built the first *kaisho* that was a separate building, and from then on each shogun who lived in the Muromachi Palace built his own *kaisho*. In the days of Yoshimasa's predecessors, the *kaisho* sometimes served as the site of conferences between the shogun and his ministers, so often, in fact, that *bakufu* politics were often referred to as "*kaisho* politics."[5]

Yoshimasa, however, had no intention of using the *kaisho* at his Higashiyama retreat for political conferences with advisers. He had abdicated as shogun in order to get away from the bickering of politicians. He had hated having to listen to his advisers debate opposing views, but (because he was the shogun) he was obliged to endure the boredom. Now he was a free man. None of the retreat buildings would be used for political or other public purposes; they were variously intended instead as Yoshimasa's residence, as temple buildings where he would worship, or as rooms where he might indulge in aesthetic pursuits.[6]

The *kaisho*, was not, however, intended to be a hermitage where Yoshimasa, renouncing ties with other human beings, gave himself to solitary contemplation of the sorrows of the world. Other build-

Wooden statue of Ashikaga Yoshimasa, dressed in the robes of a Zen priest.
(Courtesy Jishō-ji, Kyoto)

Portrait of Ikkyū Sōjun by Bokusai Shōtō, Ikkyū's appointed successor and the compiler of the official chronology of Ikkyū's life. (Courtesy Tokyo National Museum)

Portrait of Ashikaga Yoshihisa by Kanō Masanobu. (Courtesy Jizō-in)

Interior of the Dōjinsai, a four-and-a-half-mat room where Ashikaga Yoshi-masa drank tea with friends. The square pillars, *shōji*, staggered shelves, writing desk, and tatami-covered floor would become typical of tea ceremony rooms. The garden is an integral part of the room. (Courtesy Jishō-ji, Kyoto)

ings at the Higashiyama retreat were suitable for Zen meditation or for recitation of the *nenbutsu*, but the *kaisho* provided the pleasure of human company that even a recluse sometimes desires.

Yoshimasa invited to the *kaisho* men like himself who could quietly appreciate paintings and other works of art and who were devoted to such refined activities as the composition of poetry and the formal drinking of tea. Poetry making was probably the main purpose of the *kaisho*.

Yoshimasa was an accomplished *waka* poet. He probably first learned how to compose *waka* as a small boy, as *waka* composition, along with calligraphy, was a basic part of his education. Like the Heian aristocrats, the military rulers of Japan considered the ability to produce a poem whenever the circumstances required one to be an indispensable social accomplishment. Even though relatively few poems by Yoshimasa have survived, we may assume that during his lifetime he composed a great many.

The poetic style favored by Yoshimasa (and by most poets of his day) was that of the Nijō school. Those who followed the traditions of this school believed that the most important task for a poet when composing *waka* was to express himself with simplicity and clarity. He also had to observe with great care the rules of *waka* composition that had evolved over the centuries. Allusion to the poetry of the past was considered to be essential. For this reason, an aspiring *waka* poet, regardless of his school, had to be thoroughly acquainted with the major anthologies of *waka* poetry and was expected not only to refer to older poems but also to restrict himself to their vocabulary. At all costs, he had to avoid anything that might make his poems seem ugly, whether because of words that were not in the approved poetic diction or allusions that seemed inappropriate.

Poetry making was essentially a social activity. No doubt many poets polished their verses in the solitude of their quarters, but beginning in the Heian period, members of the court were accustomed to participate in poem competitions known as *uta-awase*.

Two "teams" of poets were required to prepare poems on set top-ics, and a judge decided which side was the more successful or whether there was a tie. Strict rules of composition were formu-lated for the *uta-awase*. Although these rules are apt to seem trivial and even arbitrary, they imparted literary value to what might oth-erwise have been no more than a game. Without rules, there would have been no objective way of deciding which of two similar *waka* on a given theme was superior. The judge of an *uta-awase* had to be a recognized expert, familiar with all the rules; otherwise, his deci-sion on the relative merits of two poems might become an occasion for recriminations. Only a master of the art could be sure that his decisions would be accepted without dispute.

Yoshimasa seems to have enjoyed taking part in *uta-awase* ses-sions. It is hard to imagine that any judge would have dared not to award the palm to a *waka* composed by the shogun, but surviving examples indicate that even without benefit of favoritism, Yoshimasa could have held his own. He was familiar enough with the rules of poetry to avoid committing any obvious fault, and even though his poems are seldom memorable, he took poetry making seriously.

Yoshimasa's private collection of *waka* includes a poetic dialogue between him and Asukai Masachika, a poet who often served as a judge of *uta-awase*. Before quoting a *waka* by Masachika, Yoshi-masa wrote the following headnote:

When I sent Asukai Masamichi one hundred poems I had myself composed and asked him to rate them, he affixed his seal of approval to fifty-two of them, then wrote at the end of the scroll,

momokusa ni	None of the hundred
niowanu iro wa	Grasses is without fragrance,
nakeredomo	But I gaze with even
hana aru wo koso	Greater, unending pleasure
nao akazu mireō	On those that bear flowers.

In reply, Yoshimasa sent a poem in which he declared that his "flowers," poor things though they were, had come from the heart.[7]

Yoshimasa's *waka* rarely displayed the individuality we might expect of so unusual a man, but his "poems of complaint" (*jukkai*) are sometimes effective. The following poem suggests dissatisfaction with himself and hints at his difficulty in governing the country:

ukiyo zo to	"What a sad world it is!"
nabete iedomo	Everyone says the same, but
osameenu	I'm the only one,
wagami hitotsu ni	Unable to control it,
nao nageku kana	Whose grief keeps on growing.[8]

Yoshimasa also wrote some poetry in Chinese. The Higashiyama period was one of the high points—perhaps the highest—of the composition of *kanshi* in Japan.[9] Many of the best *kanshi* were written by Zen monks attached to one of the Five Mountains (*gozan*), the major Zen monasteries in Kyoto. Yoshimasa had frequent contacts with these monks and undoubtedly knew their poetry and sometimes joined with them in composing *kanshi*, but he was more interested in *waka* than in *kanshi*. After Shōtetsu's death in 1459, there were no outstanding *waka* poets for Yoshimasa to emulate, but this probably did not disturb him. Poets who occupy only a minor place in the history of *waka* were important in their day, and Yoshimasa turned to them for comments and praise.

The most important form of Japanese poetry in the Higashiyama culture was undoubtedly *renga*. During the first centuries of its existence (the oldest example goes back to the eighth century), *renga* was little more than a test of whether a second poet was clever enough to complete a poem after someone else had composed a puzzling seventeen syllables. The more obscure the opening verse, the greater the achievement of the man who managed to make sense of it in his response. Sometimes, as in the following example, four-teen syllables were followed by seventeen:

abunaku mo ari	It is frightening
medetaku mo ari	But also brings us joy
muko iri no	The log bridge
yube ni wataru	We cross in the evening
hitotsubashi	To welcome the groom.[10]

The first verse presents the elements of a riddle: What is at once dangerous and felicitous? The answer: the members of a family cross a shaky single-log bridge to welcome the young man they will take into their family. The reply to the puzzling first link was clever, but the exchange does not make a satisfactory whole. *Renga* was still hardly more than a game.

The breakthrough in the creation of *renga* as a serious poetic art occurred when sequences in more than two links came into fashion at the end of the twelfth century. The "chain *renga*" (*kusari renga*), as it was called, developed eventually into a long poem composed by several persons responding by turns to one another's "links" in accordance with rules evolved by poets at the court. Sensing the literary possibilities of a poetic form that had previously been mainly a display of quick wit, they gave it dignity by providing it with rules.

Nijō Yoshimoto (1320–1388) was the first to write perceptively of the art of the *renga*. He considered it to be a form of *waka*, thereby exalting it to the level of a sacred art. The distinctive feature of *renga* at this time, apart from the fact that a single poem was composed by several poets, was that its language was not restricted to the poetic vocabulary of the imperially sponsored collections. It also could be more contemporary in subject matter, sometimes touching on current situations rather than the eternal themes preferred by *waka* poets in the bulk of their poems. *Minase sangin* (*Three Poets at Minase*), the most famous *renga* sequence, includes this link by Sōgi, the great master of *renga*, evoking the misery of Kyoto during the Ōnin War:

kusaki sae	Even plants and trees
furuki miyako no	Share the bitter memories
urami ni te	Of the old capital.[11]

The rules of *renga* multiplied in the attempt to make a game into a refined literary art. Finally, so many rules were created that there was a need for specialists who knew them all, and sessions of *renga* were presided over by experts who were ready to disqualify a link if it broke even the most obscure rule.

The art of *renga* reached its height during the late fifteenth century. The two greatest poets of *renga*—Sōgi (1421–1502) and Shinkei (1406–1475)—were active at this time, and other poets of almost equal distinction took part with them in creating *renga* sequences in a hundred or even a thousand links. *Renga* were composed not just by the relatively few masters but by innumerable people all over the country, including illiterates, as we can infer from these remarks by Shinkei:

The *renga* verses I have heard recently in country districts have none of the earmarks of a disciplined, conscious art. The poets seem to be in a state of complete confusion. Indeed, ever since amateurs have grown so numerous the art of composing noble, deeply felt poetry seems to have come to an end. *Renga* has become nothing more than a glib chattering, and all mental discipline has vanished without a trace. That is why when one passes along the roads or by the marketplaces one's ears are assaulted by the sounds of thousand-verse or ten-thousand-verse compositions, and even the rare persons who have real familiarity with the art employ it solely as a means of earning a living. Day after day, night after night, they engage in indiscriminate composition together. Our times would seem to correspond to the age of stultification and final decline of the art.[12]

Why, one may wonder, was *renga* so popular in the Higashiyama era? The simplest answer, though it is difficult to prove, is that at a time of warfare and hostilities that separated man from man, *renga* was popular because it brought people together in convivial circumstances. From this time, there are frequent mentions of friends gathering to eat a simple meal and then enjoying the pleasure of composing *renga* or *waka* together. Or the same people might, after drinking saké, sing ballads to dissipate the gloom of their daily lives. In the midst of the violent conflicts of the Ōnin War, people yearned for and found comradeship and peace in such gatherings. As Haga Kōshirō wrote, "Communality was definitely one of the notable characteristics of the Higashiyama culture.[13]

Renga was ideal entertainment for a small group of friends who gathered in an evening in what may have seemed like an island of peace and goodwill, the spiritual refuge of each. By its very nature, a *renga* session was not a suitable place for controversy. A clash of political views or of economic interests would fatally impair the harmony necessary for men who gathered to create *renga* together. In the interests of harmony, certain subjects were banned from the conversation at these gatherings, including discussions of politics or religion, mention of household matters, and criticism of other people.[14]

Unlike the *uta-awase*, which pitted one poet against another, each competing for recognition as superior to the other, *renga* was a cooperative effort. It was rather like the ancient *kemari* (kickball), a game in which the players do not attempt to kick the ball so far that no one can retrieve it or to kick it into a net in order to win a point. Instead, they help one other in keeping the ball from falling to the ground; there is no competition and no winner. The same is true of *renga*. A participant in a *renga* session who tried to prove that he was better at composing *renga* than anybody else, in this way destroying the unity of mood that the other poets were trying to create, would not be invited to another session.

The participants often thought of themselves as belonging to a *za*, a group of people who shared a communality of spirit. This did not necessarily involve any loss of individuality by the members of the *za*, though it is true that nobody deliberately tried to be unlike the others. Nijō Yoshimoto compared *renga* with nō, another art perpetuated by a *za*. The nō actors who perform a play belong to the same *za* and are accustomed to working with and supporting one another, but this does not include suppressing their individual characteristics as actors. The ideal members of a *renga* session were men who knew one another well and could respond easily to one another's poems but who never merely echoed.

The art of *renga* was so highly esteemed that some thought it partook of the divine. In 1471 a *hokku* (the opening verse of a *renga* sequence) offered by Sōgi to the Mishima Shrine in Izu was credited with effecting the miraculous cure of a child. And in 1504 Sōgi's disciple Sōchō offered at the same shrine a *renga* sequence in a thousand links by way of prayer for the victory in battle of the daimyo he served.

No doubt participants in the *renga* sequences composed by amateurs in the countryside, the kind of poets for whom Shinkei displayed contempt, sometimes forgot the spirit of joint composition and contributed a verse that brought momentary applause, even if it broke the rules. The kind of *renga* practiced by Sōgi, Shinkei, and their peers was too lofty for average amateurs to approximate, but amateurs were just as eager as the masters to take part in *renga*, crude though their compositions might be.

It is not surprising that Shinkei, a consecrated poet of *renga*, should have looked with disdain on ignorant merchants and farmers who thought they were composing *renga*. But however much contempt *renga* masters might express in their writings for would-be poets who did not understand the higher reaches of the art, not even they could be wholly free of worldly concerns. The disorder and destruction during the Ōnin War caused many *renga* poets to flee the capital and look for patrons elsewhere. Daimyos and other rich men in remote parts of the country, eager to become proficient in composing the kind of poetry most in vogue in the capital, gladly offered *renga* masters hospitality in return for receiving guidance in composing *renga*.

Composing *renga* in the style of Sōgi was exhausting for daimyos, who were primarily fighting men and not poets. However eager they may have been to become proficient in the serious *renga*, they must have breathed a sigh of relief when the serious session ended and refreshments were served. Then the participants could unbend and indulge themselves in comic, or even ribald, *renga* sequences.

Ashikaga Yoshimasa was devoted to *renga* composition. Early in his reign as shogun, he sponsored an annual *renga* session in a thousand links at the Kitano Shrine, and on numerous other occasions he joined guests in composing *renga*. In the spring of 1465, when he was in his thirtieth year, he visited various sites in the city famed for their cherry blossoms, then at their height. Afterward, a *renga* session was held at Kachōyama, one of the Higashiyama hills.[15] Of course, Yoshimasa was asked to compose the *hokku*, considered to be the most important. He wrote:

> *sakimichite*   Flowers in full bloom—
> *hana yori hoka no*   But apart from the blossoms,
> *iro mo nashi*   No color anywhere.

Two days later, on an excursion to Oharano, he composed the *hokku* at another *renga* gathering:

tōku kite	It was worth having
miru kai ari ya	Come from afar to behold
sakurabana	Cherries in full bloom

These *hokku* convey Yoshimasa's pleasure on seeing the masses of cherry blossoms. Perhaps the former implies that there was little to cheer one's eyes apart from the blossoms, but this was a relatively happy year for Yoshimasa. When he went to see the blossoms at Kachōyama, he was accompanied by his wife, Hino Tomiko, who would give birth in the eleventh month of that year to his first son, Yoshihisa. In the eighth month, Yoshimasa went to Higashiyama, perhaps already thinking of building a retreat there.

When Yoshimasa decided to build the *kaisho* at his mountain retreat, he probably was anticipating the pleasure of composing *renga* with friends in those surroundings. The gardens and hills visible from the *kaisho* would provide inspiration for the poetry. At some point in the gathering, food and drink would be served, strengthening the feeling of belonging to a *za* of like-minded friends. Even the most skillful who participated in the session of *renga* probably did not consider themselves to be the equals of Sōgi or Shinkei, and that may be why none of the texts of the poems composed on such occasions survive. The "links" of the *renga* sequence may have been written down by a scribe, in the manner of the sessions of professional *renga* poets, but the manuscripts seem not to have been treasured. The participants were probably pleased to think of themselves as amateurs, gentlemen of leisure who composed verses as a pleasure shared with intimates; they had no ambition of creating immortal poetry. In this sense, these men were the prototypes of the *bunjin*, the gentlemen-poets of the Edo period, an ideal for which the original inspiration came from China.

It is not clear which guests Yoshimasa invited to the *kaisho* to enjoy one another's company and to share the pleasure of composing poetry, casually sketching, and drinking saké or tea together. Probably they included nobles and cultivated members of the military class but not Zen priests from the Kyoto monasteries, even though Yoshimasa enjoyed a friendly association with them. As Haga Kōshirō wrote, "The Zen priests were extremely skillful at composing linked verse in Chinese, but they were completely uninterested in composing *renga*; I have yet to find an example from a reliable source of a Zen priest who composed *renga*."[16]

Yoshimasa worshiped Chinese culture, as we know from his collection of paintings and other works of art. He read not only those Chinese classics that were known to every educated Japanese of the time but less familiar works as well that he ordered from China. Reading even fairly difficult texts in Chinese was probably no problem for Yoshimasa. Chinese was probably as familiar to him as Latin was to the European intellectuals who, over centuries, composed both poetry and scientific treatises in Latin and assumed that every educated person would be able to read them. But however competent the Japanese might become in composing poems in Chinese, they could not totally forsake the customs of their own country. I find it difficult, for example, to imagine Yoshimasa and his friends seated on chairs (as Chinese would have done) while they composed *renga*. Also, the topics of Yoshimasa's *waka* were unmistakably Japanese, in the tradition of the Heian poets, and seldom borrowed from Chinese poetry. Although his poems do not rank as masterpieces, the language reveals, as in this *waka* on plovers (*chidori*), how sensitive Yoshimasa was to the music of Japanese:

tsuki nokoru	How the plovers rise up
urawa no nami no	When they see the vestiges
shinonome ni	Of the moon lingering
omokage miete	At the break of day
*tatsu chidori kan*a	In the waves off the shore.[17]

8

Ashikaga Yoshimasa's mountain retreat at Higashiyama was a realization of aesthetic concepts he had
formed after losing interest in worldly ambition. At
the retreat, he was surrounded by beauty in the natural surroundings and in the art with which he filled
the buildings. Apart from the paintings he commis-
sioned (like the *fusuma-e* of Kanō Masanobu), the
works of art collected and displayed were mostly
paintings and ceramics imported from China. The
rooms must have produced an impression quite
unlike those of earlier palaces.

The extent of the change can be measured in
terms of the differences in the ways in which works
of art were displayed in a Heian palace room and in
the Higashiyama retreat. The typical art of the Heian

period was *emakimono* (horizontal scroll paintings) and *shōji-e* (*fusuma* paintings). An *emakimono*, normally not on display, was taken from wherever it was stored and viewed by unrolling it with both hands on a flat surface. The *shōji-e* consisted of paintings on walls, *fusuma*, folding screens, and single-leaf screens that were part of a room's permanent decorations. They always were visible and could not easily be changed to match the season or some special occasion.

From the middle of the Kamakura period, many *kakemono* (hanging scroll paintings) had been imported from China. They were difficult to display in rooms of traditional Japanese architecture because there was no suitable place to hang them. Even if there was wall space, a *kakemono* looked naked against a wall with nothing (like the frame of a European painting) to set it off. Accordingly, it eventually became customary to place on the floor beneath a *kakemono* a table on which objects of art such as an incense burner, a flower vase, or candlesticks might be displayed. These objects helped create a defined space for the pictures.

The next step in establishing a place within a room where paintings and objects of art could be effectively displayed came when the table, no longer freestanding, was attached to the wall below the *kakemono*, forming a kind of shelf. This shelf, known as an *oshiita*, provided a base for the painting and could also be used as a stand on which to display objects of art.

The *oshiita* was twelve to eighteen feet in width and about one foot in depth. Its disproportionate width, compared with its shallow depth, was dictated by the Chinese custom of hanging three related *kakemono* side by side, requiring an *oshiita* wide enough to serve as a base for all three.

The *oshiita* was the ancestor of the *tokonoma* (alcove), which first appeared in the Higashiyama era. The *tokonoma*, quite differently proportioned from the *oshiita*, had vertical columns, often slender tree trunks, that further served to frame the paintings and other objects displayed. The *tokonoma* became an indispensable element in every Japanese room in which guests were entertained. From time to time, Yoshimasa probably changed the paintings and objects of art on display in order to share with his guests the many different works in his collection of Chinese art.

Among the Chinese ceramics frequently displayed on the *oshiita* were flower vases. Japanese had undoubtedly been putting flowers into vases for a very long time. As far back as the seventh century (the Nara period), people had offered flowers in containers to the gods and buddhas. Apparently, though, it was not considered necessary to arrange the flowers artistically, the manner of presentation being far less important than the flowers offered.

During the Heian period, the beauty of flowers was often mentioned by poets, but they wrote mainly about flowers in gardens rather than in vases. During the Kamakura and early Muromachi periods, flower vases imported from China were prized as superb examples of ceramic art, but they were not necessarily used to contain flowers. Even when flowers were placed in the vases, they apparently were thrust in without trying to achieve an artistic effect. Until the Higashiyama period, no one seems to have given much thought to the most effective and beautiful way of displaying flowers.[1]

Not until Yoshimasa's time was it realized that flowers in a vase could be elevated to a form of art, a discovery that gave rise to the art of flower arrangement (*kadō*). Once the arrangement of flowers acquired the credentials of an art, its function was debated by practitioners. Some insisted that the center of attention must be the flowers and that the beauty of the vase was only incidental. Others were equally sure that the flowers served merely to enhance the beauty of the vase.[2] Other disputes revolved around such points as whether only beautiful flowers were suitable for arrangements or whether humble plants and grasses also deserved a place in a vase.

The rooms at the Higashiyama palace were decorated with floral displays intended to harmonize with the paintings. The colors and sizes of the flowers were chosen to keep them from clashing with the paintings, an indication that despite the new prominence of floral display, paintings continued to be considered the primary decorations of a room. We can infer this also from *Kundaikan sō chōki*, the catalogue of Chinese paintings in the shogun's collection. Although Nōami, the author, was known not only for his connoisseurship but also for his skill in displaying paintings, he offered no guidance as to how flowers were to be arranged in conjunction with paintings.

Probably the flower arrangements in Yoshimasa's palace were *tatebana* (standing flowers, known today as *rikka*). The oldest surviving account of someone arranging flowers at the court is dated April 20, 1476. On that day, Yoshimasa, accompanied by Hino Tomiko and Yoshihisa, visited the imperial palace. The account states that Yoshimasa asked Ryūami (one of his *dōbōshū*) to "stand" some peonies.[3] Later on, there are frequent mentions in *Inryōken nichiroku*[4] of Ryūami's having "stood flowers," and he is now honored as one of the first masters of the art of flower arrangement.

An entry in the same chronicle for the second month of 1486 describes how Kisen Shūshō, a priest of the Shōkoku-ji, offered Yoshimasa a branch of pale red plum blossoms, a branch of deep red plum blossoms, and several sprays of narcissus. Yoshimasa, pleased with the gift, sent for Ryūami, intending to ask him to arrange the flowers. But Ryūami declined to appear, pleading that he was ill. Possibly his reluctance to obey the shogun's command was caused by fear that his arrangement of such an unusual combination of flowers might not meet with the shogun's approval. Yoshimasa was insistent. He ordered Ryūami to come before him, regardless of his illness, and when Ryūami appeared, he commanded him to arrange the flowers. Ryūami's arrangement was so successful that the delighted Yoshimasa bestowed on him a quantity of saké. It has been said that Ryūami's success on this occasion first brought him fame as a flower arranger, but it is more likely, in view of Yoshimasa's insistence that Ryūami (and nobody else) arrange the flowers, that he was already recognized as an expert.

The anecdote demonstrates that Yoshimasa was not satisfied if the flowers he received were merely thrust into a vase, that he believed that skill in arranging the flowers enhanced their natural beauty. When it became known that Yoshimasa was pleased to receive gifts of flowers, those seeking his favor offered him huge bouquets. But Yoshimasa preferred simple arrangements in the *rikka* style to masses of blossoms.[5]

The invention of the *rikka* style of arranging flowers is generally credited not to Ryūami but to Senkei, a member of the Ikenobō school of flower arrangers who, not content with merely putting flowers together in a pleasing mixture of shapes and colors, created in 1462 this distinctive style of arrangement. Senkei explained his manner of arranging flowers in terms of the symbolic Buddhist interpretation he gave to each of the seven "branches" of his arrangements. By providing a code for *rikka*, he elevated flower arrangement into a "Way" (*michi*), much in the manner that *renga* and other arts of the Muromachi period, originally no more than entertainments, were given importance and dignity by the creation of codes. The success of Senkei's innovative flower arrangements brought a popularity to the Ikenobō school that it has retained to this day.

The remarkable ability that the Japanese display in arranging flowers artistically is today recognized throughout the world. Many people in foreign countries (mainly women) diligently study and practice the art under Japanese masters, hoping that one day they will become proficient and be rewarded with an artistic name. It is by no means easy to arrange flowers so skillfully as to gain the respect of a master, and foreigners who have trouble absorbing the principles sometimes conclude that the ability to arrange flowers is inborn in the Japanese and perhaps impossible for non-Japanese to learn. However, the skill the Japanese display in making arrangements that are at once natural looking and yet seem to evoke an abstract world of beauty is achieved only after study. Like much else that falls under the heading of the "soul of Japan," flower arrangement had its inception not in the ancient past of the Japanese people but in Yoshimasa's day.

Although Yoshimasa took pleasure in flower arrangements, he probably was even more interested in gardens and devoted his energies to creating gardens at his different residences, especially at Higashiyama. Once he had decided to spend his declining years in Higashiyama, he resolved that his retreat must accord exactly with his tastes, and this determination enabled him to surmount whatever obstacles he encountered.

The first obstacle was the dispute over ownership of the land where Yoshimasa planned to build his retreat. It had been the property of the Jōdo-ji, a subtemple of the Tendai monastery Enryaku-ji. Because the Jōdo-ji had been destroyed during the Ōnin War, the priests of the Enryaku-ji were planning to use the land for a cemetery. Yoshimasa, paying no attention to their protests, confiscated the property without further discussion. The priests of the Enryaku-ji appealed to Yoshimasa's son, the shogun Yoshihisa, declaring that because the site was of such great holiness, if Yoshimasa destroyed the cemetery in order to build a place merely for his recreation, his deed would surely be punished by the Buddha. Yoshihisa judged that their protest was reasonable, but in reply he informed them that his father was old and did not have much longer to live. He urged them to wait patiently during the short time until his death when the issue could be settled peaceably. (Yoshimasa at the time was forty-nine and had another seven years to live.)

Despite the opposition from the Enryaku-ji priests, Yoshimasa probably insisted on this particular spot for his retreat because the combination of flat land with nearby mountains (unlike other sites in the Higashiyama area) was ideal for the creation of gardens.

In his monumental *Higashiyama bunka no kenkyū*, Haga Kōshirō wrote about Yoshimasa: "One thing ran through his entire life and served the function of an axis to his aesthetic life: it was gardens."[6] Yoshimasa's passion for gardens had earlier been revealed in the gardens of the palaces constructed by his command in the city, but his crowning achievement as a planner of gardens was at Higashiyama. His enthusiasm for gardens coincided with a general emergence of interest in the art of landscape gardening and provided a powerful stimulus for the development of this interest. Yoshimasa not only supervised the building of his own gardens but, when he visited other gardens on his travels, often volunteered advice on improvements.

Gardens, of course, already had a long history in Japan, as we know from *The Tale of Genji* and other examples of court fiction. We are told of spring and autumn gardens, planted according to the preference of the lady who occupied an apartment overlooking a particular garden. It was believed that a garden was capable of giving not only aesthetic pleasure but also spiritual enlightenment. The prevailing religious background of the Heian garden was that of Pure Land Buddhism, especially in the emphasis on the "pity of things" (*mono no aware*), as exemplified by the perishability of the flowers and, indeed, all beauty in this world.

From the late Kamakura period, however, the cultural influence of Zen Buddhism became paramount in the planning of gardens. Celebrated Zen priests such as Musō Soseki (1275–1351) believed that gardens could serve as inspiration for Zen contemplation. This was particularly true of the rock and sand (*karesansui*) gardens, created at this time in Zen monasteries. They contained few or no flowers, perhaps because the planners wished to prevent beholders from being distracted by temporary beauty. The symbolic beauty of *yūgen*, as it is represented in such gardens, was intended to lift the beholder's mind into higher realms of understanding.

The actual construction of the gardens—the moving of rocks from distant places to particular places in a new garden, the planting of trees, and so on—was naturally not done by Yoshimasa's intimates but by "people of the riverbed" (*kawaramono*), the lowest class of society. Although these people performed many necessary services, they suffered extreme discrimination, in part at least because they were traditionally associated with the slaughter of beasts, a loathsome occupation to Buddhists. Even though warriors protected themselves with armor made of leather, they felt only contempt or even revulsion for the *kawaramono* who had killed the animals and treated their skins to make leather. The government did not permit *kawaramono* to live in the same areas as other Japanese but allowed them to build their huts only in such unappealing places as the dried bed (*kawara*) of the Kamo River in Kyoto, which, because it was underwater for part of the year, did not belong to anyone.

The *kawaramono* who first took part in the construction of gardens probably performed only manual labor under the direction of the Zen priests who had planned the gardens. However, as the result of spending many hours moving earth and trees, they gained a practical knowledge of the art of building gardens. Eventually, their skill at creating gardens was recognized by the priests and by the shogun himself.[7]

The *kawaramono* felt confident of Yoshimasa's protection. When Yoshimasa sent a group of *kawaramono* gardeners to the Ichijō-in, a subtemple of the Kōfuku-ji in Nara, to obtain trees for his gardens, the monks were extremely irritated by the presence in their temple of members of the lowest social class who walked around with an air that suggested they owned the place. The priests also disliked being obliged to offer these people food, drink, and money solely because they had come at Yoshimasa's behest. Although they had no choice but to give Yoshimasa the trees he wanted, they refused to allow the *kawaramono* to inspect them and forced them to return to Kyoto.

Yoshimasa was furious over the priests' actions. By way of retaliation, he ordered the shogunate to confiscate some of their estates.

The alarmed head of the Ichijō-in asked the nobleman Konoe Masaie (1444–1505), the *dajō daijin* (prime minister), to convey the temple's profound apologies. Masaie in turn sent an envoy to Ise Sadachika begging him to use his good offices to promote a reconciliation. Yoshimasa accepted the priests' apology, and the *kawaramono* went back to Nara to inspect the gardens of the Ichijō-in, this time without fear of interruption.[8]

Among the *kawaramono* experts on gardens, Yoshimasa relied most on Zen'ami, who died in 1482 in his ninety-seventh year. Although Zen'ami belonged to a class that was despised by most Japanese, Yoshimasa seems to have been free of prejudice. When, for example, Zen'ami was stricken with a serious illness in 1460, the anxious Yoshimasa asked the high-ranking priest Kikei Shinzui to prepare a special medicine for him and gave orders that he be kept informed daily of the state of Zen'ami's illness. Indeed, Yoshimasa had such a high opinion of Zen'ami that he seems to have feared that if he died, there would be no one to create gardens after his tastes. Fortunately, Zen'ami recovered on this occasion, but other entries in *Inryōken nichiroku* mention Yoshimasa's repeated show of concern for Zen'ami's health.

Even after Zen'ami had become an extremely old man, each time he was stricken with illness, Yoshimasa sent medicines and prayed for his recovery. Kikei Shinzui complained about the excessively kind treatment that Yoshimasa accorded to someone of base birth, but Yoshimasa ignored his complaints. The attentions he showered on the master gardener were credited with prolonging Zen'ami's life until the ripe old age of ninety-seven, but he more likely owed his longevity to an unusually hardy physique.

Yoshimasa was generous with his rewards whenever Zen'ami had especially pleased him with some new effect. An entry in *Inryōken nichiroku* for the twelfth month of 1460 reports that Yoshimasa bestowed on Zen'ami the lavish gift of five thousand *hiki* in recognition of his accomplishments as a creator of gardens.[9]

On one occasion, Yoshimasa praised On'ami, the nō master, and "*kawaramono* Zen'ami" to Kikei Shinzui, expressing in one breath his joy that both were in good health despite their old age. His readiness to couple On'ami, Yoshinori's favorite nō actor, with a mere *kawaramono* plainly indicates how highly he esteemed Zen'ami.[10]

Haga Kōshirō likened Yoshimasa's indifference to Zen'ami's lowly status to his choice of Shōtetsu, a low-ranking priest, to deliver lectures on *The Tale of Genji*. Normally, a member of the noble Asukai family would have performed this service, but Yoshimasa had discovered Shōtetsu's exceptional literary ability and chose him as the lecturer, despite his humble rank. Again, when Yoshimasa was arranging for paintings to decorate his palaces, he passed over the traditional court painters of the Tosa family and chose instead Oguri Sōtan, whom he named his painter in residence, and Kanō Masanobu, whose paintings decorated the Higashiyama retreat. Haga interpreted these choices as examples of Yoshimasa's valuing art above every other consideration (*geijutsu shijō shugi*).[11] He was ready to favor anyone who had demonstrated that he was a master of his art.

It is hard to be sure what specifically convinced Yoshimasa that a garden constructed by Zen'ami was superior to any other. Kikei Shinzui wrote of the garden at the Suiinken within the Shōkoku-ji complex of temples: "The most extraordinary features of a garden designed by Zen'ami are the far and near, the peaks and valleys. One can never get tired of them. Before one knows it, one has forgotten to go home." Kikei also wrote, "No one can compare with his skill in building mountains and introducing water. This must be why he receives twice as much praise as anyone else."[12] These tantalizingly brief remarks suggest that Zen'ami may have conceived of his gardens much in the manner of a *bonseki*, creating in a restricted space the illusion of sweeping landscapes of mountains and rivers. This intent accorded with the power of suggestion that

Yoshimasa prized in the arts—whether nō, architecture, or flower arrangement—and ultimately may be traced back to his familiarity with Zen aesthetics.

The death of Zen'ami in 1482, just as work was to begin on the Higashiyama retreat, deprived Yoshimasa of his most trusted adviser on gardens. Zen'ami had earlier planned the gardens of the Inryōken at the Shōkoku-ji, the water garden at the Palace of Flowers, the garden at the Takakura Palace, and the garden of the Daijō-in at the Kōfuku-ji in Nara, where he took refuge during the Ōnin War. His fees for constructing these gardens were high,[13] but his customers—the shogun and major monasteries—did not doubt that they received their money's worth.

Who could possibly succeed Zen'ami? Considering how extremely old he was at the end, surely Yoshimasa must have given thought to his successor. Whoever was chosen, the task ahead would be daunting: to plan and supervise the construction of the gardens of the Higashiyama retreat, the site of the final flowering of Yoshimasa's aesthetic tastes. It is not certain who actually was chosen to succeed Zen'ami. For many years, it was believed that the architect of the Higashiyama gardens was Sōami, the most distinguished of Yoshimasa's *dōbōshū*, but this theory has been discarded if only because Sōami is not known to have shown any special interest in gardens.[14]

Zen'ami's son, Koshirō, and his grandson, Matashirō, were probably the most qualified to succeed him.[15] Both had worked with Zen'ami, and Matashirō had demonstrated special ability. Yoshimasa seems to have decided that Matashirō was more talented than his father and appointed him to succeed Zen'ami, but there is no clear proof.[16]

After examining the evidence concerning who deserved credit for creating the Higashiyama gardens, Haga Kōshirō concluded that although it involved the cooperation of Zen priests, *kawara-mono* gardeners, and members of Yoshimasa's staff, Yoshimasa himself was the guiding spirit and deserved the chief credit.[17] Yoshimasa certainly displayed strong preferences with respect to gardens and voiced opinions concerning every aspect of the planning, but he probably was not acquainted with the physical details of creating a garden—how, for example, to place rocks, trees, and water to create an illusion of mountains or of flowing rivers. Matashirō, Zen'ami's successor, probably deserves the greatest credit, but there is not enough evidence to be sure.

The gardens of the Higashiyama mountain retreat have virtually disappeared, though perhaps some elements of the present garden of the Ginkaku-ji preserve the appearance of the originals. The garden (like that at the Takakura Palace) owed much to the garden of the Saihō-ji, planned by Musō, where the pond and the island in the pond were central elements, but the lovely setting in the Higashiyama hills gave the Ginkaku-ji its special character.

Although modern scholars pay far more attention to the buildings of the Ginkaku-ji than to the gardens, probably both were equally important to Yoshimasa. The original two-story Silver Pavilion was not intended for any specifically religious use. Instead, its main function was to provide a suitable lookout from which to gaze out on the gardens, itself a religious experience.

The Muromachi period was the golden age of Japanese gardens. The importance attached to gardens by the Zen monks accounted for the magnificent gardens at various temples, but it was Yoshimasa's love of gardens that led to the creation of some of the most beautiful ones. Few, though, survived the warfare of the sixteenth century. The two best-known gardens of the period, if only because they still may be seen, are those of the Ryōan-ji and the Daisen-in of the Daitoku-ji, gardens of sand and stones, without vegetation except for moss growing around the stones. Most likely, they were Chinese in inspiration, brought back to Japan by Zen monks. Indeed, Haga Kōshirō suggested that the term *karesansui* for waterless gardens was originally *karasansui*, or Chinese gardens.[18] The corruption in the pronunciation may have occurred unconsciously as the concept of a garden without water or plants became familiar, but perhaps the shift from *kara* (China) to *kare* (dry) was deliberate, a quiet assertion that such gardens had become thoroughly Japanese.

The sand and stone gardens were an extreme form of the tendency in Zen-inspired gardens to aim at symbolic effects rather than to serve as idealized representations of nature, in the manner of more conventional gardens. The sand garden of the Ginkaku-ji may have represented an attempt to reconcile the Zen preference for *karesansui* with the equally strong love of flowing water. Although the Zen influence is apparent in the waterless gardens, the strongest Chinese influence on Japanese gardens as a whole may have come from ink landscape paintings.

It is a unfortunate that so few gardens of Yoshimasa's time survive, but they had many progeny, scattered all over Japan.

9

Ashikaga Yoshimasa is especially associated with innovation in gardens and flower arrangement, but his appreciation of other arts helped foster their development. Among them, none is better known than *chanoyu*, perhaps the most Japanese of the traditional arts. Japanese were drinking tea well before Yoshimasa's time, but the four-and-a-half-mat room at the Ginkaku-ji where he drank tea with intimates became the model for Japanese to emulate in his time and much later. Yoshimasa gave the authority of the shogunate to what had been no more than an elegant pastime and led the way to the ritualized consumption of tea that culminated in the *wabicha* evolved by the great Sen no Rikyū.

The drinking of tea goes back at least two thousand years. The tea plant seems to have been indigenous to Yunnan in southeastern China. Its leaves may at first have been eaten by people who had little other nourishment. In fact, tea leaves are still eaten by people in northern Thailand and elsewhere in Southeast Asia, sometimes pickled or salted. The leaves, whether eaten or (as has since become normal throughout the world) drunk after being infused in water, were believed to contain curative properties, and for many years people drank tea not for its flavor or refreshing effect but as a medicine. At first the green leaves were simply boiled in water, but then it was discovered that the taste was improved by roasting or fermenting the leaves and grinding them into powder.

The drinking of tea spread from Yunnan to Szechuan and eventually to all of China. It continued to be consumed mainly as a medicine, though tradition has it that Bodhidharma, who introduced Zen Buddhism to China in 520, recommended drinking tea because it helped people stay awake during long religious ceremonies. By the seventh century, tea drinking had become part of everyday Chinese life, and in the eighth century, the first work appeared that was dedicated entirely to a description of tea: its origins, manner of preparation, manner of drinking, and utensils used. This work, *Ch'a-ching* (*The Classic of Tea*), was written by Lu Yü (727?–804?).[1] Okakura Kakuzō derived the name of his celebrated *The Book of Tea* from Lu Yü's text, which he translated and popularized.

For Lu Yü (as for his predecessors), the chief value of tea was medicinal, and he listed various ailments that could be cured by drinking it. However, his enthusiasm for the medical properties of tea did not make him forget the pleasant effect brought about by drinking four or five cups of tea. Lu Yü even claimed that tea rivaled *daigo* and *kanro*, beverages famed since antiquity for their delicious taste.[2]

Tea was introduced to Japan from China as part of the widespread adoption of the continent's superior culture. The first unmistakable mention of tea in a Japanese document is in an entry for 815 in the *Nihon kōki*, one of the Six Dynastic Histories. The entry, describing the visit of Emperor Saga to Karasaki on the shore of Lake Biwa, relates that when the emperor's palanquin reached the Sūfuku-ji, he got out, went into the temple, and worshiped the Buddha. Next, he visited the Bonshaku-ji where, stopping the palanquin, he sang a poem in Chinese. Those accompanying him joined in poetic composition, and the abbot Eichū offered the emperor tea that he himself had brewed.[3]

Eichū spent thirty years in China, from 775 to 805, just about the time when Lu Yü was writing his *Classic of Tea*, but there is no evidence that they were acquainted. When Eichū, who had evidently acquired a taste for tea, returned to Japan, he took tea with him. Two months after drinking the tea prepared by Eichū, Emperor Saga, who all but worshiped Chinese culture, had tea bushes planted in the area of the capital and commanded that tea be presented to him every year. Tea bushes were planted even within the precincts of the imperial palace.

Tea is mentioned (under the name *ryokumei* [green tea]) in the *Bunka shūrei shū*, the collection of *kanshi* compiled in 818 during the reign of Emperor Saga.[4] When, however, the ardor for Chinese culture diminished and the embassies to China were discontinued on the recommendation of Sugawara no Michizane, the interest in tea also waned. Despite its auspicious beginning under Saga, tea drinking lost its popularity for about three hundred years, though it never disappeared completely from Japanese life. Kumakura Isao associated this loss with the discontinuation of the habit of drinking milk. Ninth-century Japanese records contain numerous references to drinking not only tea but also milk. The practice of diluting tea with milk, widespread in India and in many countries of Central Asia, probably existed in Japan. But mentions of milk drinking gradually disappear from Japanese records, and not until the Edo period were milk products used in Japan again.[5] No reason has been given for the loss of popularity except for the unexplained observation that milk did not suit the Japanese taste.

Whatever the reason, tea agreed with the Japanese better than milk did, but the revival of interest in tea had to wait for centuries for the priest Yōsai (also known as Eisai) to reintroduce the beverage. The tea he brought to Japan from China, unlike the variety earlier introduced to Japan, was not fermented but kept its fresh flavor. The Japanese preferred it to the tea they had previously consumed, and Yōsai ranks as one of the heroes in the saga of tea drinking in Japan.

Yōsai was born in 1141. As a boy of thirteen, he climbed Mount Hiei, where he was inducted as a Tendai monk. He was particularly absorbed by the Taimitsu doctrines, a variety of esoteric Buddhism founded by Ennin (794–864), who had studied in China. (Ennin recorded his experiences in China in the extraordinary *Travel Diary of a Pilgrimage to China in Search of the Law* [*Nittō Guhō Junrei Kōki*]). One of the tenets of the Taimitsu branch of Buddhism was that there was an infinite variety of ways to obtain Buddhahood in this life and body. For some people, especially those of little learning, salvation might be obtained through nothing more than the invocation of Amida Buddha. For others, notably those at the court, aesthetic refinements might equally lead to salvation. For priests, it was most suitable to study the two mandalas and to be inducted into the esoteric teachings. But all means were legitimate and effective in obtaining salvation.

Not content with what he was able to learn in Japan, Yōsai decided to go to China for further study. In 1168, at the age of twenty-seven, he sailed from Hakata for Ningpo, for centuries the port where arriving Japanese travelers customarily entered China. Yōsai remained in China for only six months during this first visit. Although he probably drank tea on many occasions during his stay, he did not bring back tea plants or seeds when he returned to Japan.

Yōsai went to China again in 1187. He originally intended to travel beyond China, all the way to India, in order to worship at sites associated with the historical Buddha, but he was discouraged by Chinese officials who informed him that they could not guarantee his safety on what was sure to be a perilous journey. Yōsai had to be satisfied with climbing Mount T'ien-t'ai, the sacred mountain of Tendai Buddhism. In 1191, the year before he returned to Japan, Yōsai sent to Japan seedlings of the *bodaiju* (bo tree) and also of tea plants.[6] The tea plants, at first planted in northern Kyūshū, grew well in Japan, and ten or so years later some plants were sent to Toganoo near Kyoto, where they flourished.

Yōsai is best known as the author of *Kissa yōjōki* (*Drink Tea and Prolong Life*), the first draft of which was written in 1211. Three years later, Yōsai produced a revised version that he offered to the youthful shogun Minamoto Sanetomo. The *Azuma kagami* (*Mirror of the East*) relates how when suffering from a hangover, Sanetomo sent for Yōsai and asked him to say prayers for his recovery. Yōsai, of a pragmatic turn of mind, instead urged Sanetomo to drink tea, which, he said, was more effective than prayers in curing hangovers. The preface to his work opens,

> Tea is the most wonderful medicine for nourishing one's health; it is the secret of long life. On the hillsides it grows up as the spirit of the soil. Those who pick and use it are certain to attain great age. India and China both value it highly, and in the past our country too once showed a great liking for tea. Now as then it possesses the same rare qualities, and we should make wider use of it. . . .
>
> Of all the things that Heaven has created, man is the most noble. To preserve one's life so as to make the most of one's allotted span is prudent and proper. The basis of preserving life is the cultivation of health, and the secret of health lies in the well-being of the five organs. Among these five the heart is sovereign. . . . The heart is the sovereign of the five organs, tea is the chief of bitter foods, and bitter is the chief of the tastes. For this reason the heart loves bitter things, and when it is doing well all the other organs are properly regulated.[7]

Yōsai elucidated in these terms the medicinal value of tea. He gave detailed attention to the correct manner of preparing the tea leaves for drinking, a procedure that is strikingly similar to the way green tea is drunk today in Japan. Yōsai believed that tea should be strong and that, although it was permissible to drink tea whenever one felt like it, the best time was after meals, much as it is today. However, Yōsai devoted surprisingly little attention to the pleasure of drinking tea.

The cultivation of tea plants steadily increased in the years after Yōsai presented *Drink Tea and Prolong Life* to Sanetomo. Tea was planted at the Kōfuku-ji in Nara and notably at the Saidai-ji, where the tea ceremony, distinctive in its use of extremely large cups, was created and has been maintained to this day. Gradually the nature of the appeal of tea shifted from its medicinal value to its pleasure as a beverage. An ability to appreciate superior varieties of tea developed into the kind of special knowledge that marks the connoisseurship that is a part of every art in Japan. In order to prove one's ability to discriminate among varieties of tea, ranging from the best to the worst, one might have to submit to tests of skill, much as the "blind testing" of wine is performed today. This in turn led to betting on the ability of different experts to recognize a particular variety. Betting and gambling on tea testing, like betting on a person's skill in composing *renga*, became so common that in the *Kenmu shikimoku* (*Kenmu Code*), promulgated by Ashikaga Takauji in 1336 after overthrowing the government of Emperor Go-Daigo, there appears the following item:

Article 2. The need for suppressing drinking in crowds and carousing. As stated in the imperial supplementary laws, these must be strictly controlled. This also applies to gambling and to excessive sporting with women. In addition, large wagers are made at tea parties and linked-verse meetings, and incalculable sums of money are lost in this way.[8]

Ashikaga Yoshimitsu's reign as shogun was marked by a fondness for the extravagant and unusual, known as *basara*.[9] Among the
daimyos with *basara* tastes, Sasaki Dōyo (1306–1373) was known
for the extravagance of his tea parties. The room where the tea was
consumed was decorated with imported Chinese wares, including
leopard and tiger skins, and the betting was on a large scale, with
expensive prizes for the winners. Accounts of tea parties at this
time often mention the lavish decorations in the rooms and the
elaborate manner of preparing the tea. It was a far cry from such
festive gatherings to the austerity of the tea ceremony as it developed during the fifteenth and sixteenth centuries, but it is clear
from *Kissa ōrai*, a work compiled at the end of the fourteenth century, that all the elements that would be found in the *wabicha* of Sen
no Rikyū (1522–1591) were present at the tea parties of that time.[10]

The next step in the development of what became known as
chanoyu came with the shift from the use of elaborately decorated
rooms, in which men drank saké and consumed refreshments
between bouts of tea testing and other games, to the austerity of
small, barely decorated rooms where the host and a few friends
enjoyed the pleasure of drinking tea together and quietly chatting.
The typical room where tea was consumed was in a building of the
shoin-zukuri style. The unassertive but elegant room imposed a
kind of dignity of behavior on those who drank tea, which was
probably the beginning of the *charei* (tea etiquette) that would be
so important in *wabicha*. The movements of the host as he prepared
the tea, originally casual and unpremeditated, gradually became
stylized and even beautiful, an art concealing art, and the responses
of the guests to his words and actions also were formalized to convey both respect and intimacy.

The term *chanoyu* occurs as far back as *Kyōgaku shiyō shō*, the
diary of a priest of the Kōfuku-ji in Nara, in entries dated the fifth
month of Bunmei 1 *nen* (1469).[11] This brings us to the reign as
shogun of Ashikaga Yoshimasa and the *chashitsu* (tea room) in the

Tōgu-dō at the Ginkaku-ji. Credit for having founded *sadō* (the Way of Tea) is often given to Nōami, a companion to both Yoshinori and Yoshimasa. Nōami was primarily an expert on Chinese painting (as has been noted), but he was also a skilled *renga* poet (one of the "seven sages" among Sōgi's disciples), a painter and calligrapher, and an expert blender of incense. In addition to these accomplishments, Nōami probably had his own collection of Chinese art. These factors made him an ideal practitioner of tea.

Yamanoue Sōji (1544–1590), the senior disciple in tea of Sen no Rikyū, whose *Yamanoue sōji ki* is considered to be the most authentic account of Rikyū's Way of Tea, gave an account of how Nōami first interested Yoshimasa in this art:

> Jishōin-dono [Yoshimasa] had a retreat in Higashiyama where he spent his days and nights throughout the four seasons in pleasurable diversions. Late in autumn, at a time of year when the sounds of insects on nights of waiting for the moon are most affecting, he sent for Nōami and asked him to read aloud "Judging the Qualities of Women on a Rainy Night" and other sections of *The Tale of Genji*. Nōami entertained [the shogun] with *waka*, *renga*, gazing at the moon, ball games, archery, comparing fans, naming plants, naming insects, and other diversions, and with tales of past events, whereupon Jishōin-dono said, "We have by now exhausted the usual amusements, and soon it will be winter. It would not be appropriate for someone of my age to trudge his way through snowy mountains in order to enjoy hawking. Surely there must be something else to divert us."[12]

Nōami told Yoshimasa about Shukō, a man living in Nara who had devoted himself for thirty years to the tea ceremony. He had also learned the Way of Confucius. Nōami transmitted to Yoshimasa all that he himself had learned from Shukō, including the secrets of the art of the tea ceremony. Of course, the antiques of which Yoshimasa was fond—bowls of various sizes, vases, incense burners, incense boxes, paintings, and calligraphy—were admirable in themselves, but none of them was a match for the tea ceremony, which combined them all. The calligraphy of Zen priests was particularly important to the tea ceremony. Shukō had used calligraphy by the Zen master Kango to enhance his tea ceremony, proof that Buddhist teachings could also be subsumed in tea. Adopting Nōami's suggestion, Yoshimasa sent for Shukō and appointed him as his teacher of the tea ceremony.

Kuwata Tadachika cast serious doubt on the veracity of this account. He found it impossible to believe that Yoshimasa had no acquaintance with the tea ceremony before he moved to the Higashiyama retreat. In addition, he found evidence that Yoshimasa had in fact performed *chanoyu* starting at least fifteen years earlier and even mention of a certain Mokuami, who in 1470 served Yoshimasa as "master of the tea ceremony" (*chanoyu bugyō*).[13] Kuwata guessed that Yamanoue Sōji had invented the tale of Yoshimasa's awakening to *chanoyu* in order to promote his school of *chanoyu* (and to belittle the importance of the Higashiyama *sadō*). Sōji had claimed that Shukō (and not Nōami) was Yoshimasa's teacher of *chanoyu*,[14] but Kuwata was convinced that Nōami deserved credit as both Yoshimasa's preceptor in tea and the founder of the art.

Nevertheless, there is no denying the importance of Murata Shukō (1432–1502)[15] in the development of the art of the tea ceremony. Extremely little is known about him apart from a short letter he wrote to a disciple, Furuichi Chōin (1452–1508), a feudal lord who was a practitioner of *renga*. Although the letter is difficult to understand, it is memorable for Shukō's insistence on the need "to harmonize Japanese and Chinese tastes."[16]

When speaking of Japanese taste, Shukō used such words as "cold," "withered," and "emaciated," terms borrowed from the vocabulary of *renga* criticism to indicate desirable features of the best *renga*, even though these terms were normally used in unfavorable senses. The words were especially characteristic of the *renga* criticism of Shinkei, one of the greatest of the *renga* poets, who used them to describe the qualities he sought to embody in his poetry.[17]

The closeness of the ideals of *renga* and *chanoyu* is indicative of the parallel development of the two. Like *chanoyu*, *renga* began as a test of wits, but Shinkei gave it a different dimension. He had nothing but scorn for amateur *renga* poets. When asked about the belief, common in China and in Europe, that great poetry should be intelligible even to a peasant, he replied,

> No art worthy of the name is intelligible to persons of shallow understanding who have not mastered it. No doubt even the most untalented and ignorant person may be pleased by closely related verses and a banal style, but it is inconceivable that anyone only vaguely familiar with the art could understand poetry of an elevated and profoundly beautiful nature.[18]

It can be imagined that anyone with these rather haughty views would not cater to the common preference for bright colors and a cheerful atmosphere, which may be why Shinkei found his ideals in such words as "withered," "shrunken," and "cold." In 1588, Yamanoue Sōji wrote of Shinkei, "In the *renga* criticism of Priest Shinkei, it is said that the style of *renga* should be withered, shrunken and cold. Jōō, referring to this opinion, always said that the essence of tea should be the same."[19]

Shukō's letter to Furuichi Chōin is difficult to understand because of its compression, but the meaning is roughly the following:

> In this art [*michi*] the worst thing is self-importance and egotism. To be envious of masters of the art and to look down on beginners counts as the worst kind of attitude. One should come close to the

masters and savor their every word, and one should also consider how best to train those who are still beginners. The most important thing in this art is to blend Japanese and Chinese taste. This is essential, a matter that demands the utmost care. Nowadays beginners, prattling of "cold" and "withered," covet Bizen and Shigaraki ware, a taste permissible only in masters.[20] This is unspeakably bad. By "withered" is meant possessing good utensils and fully understanding their qualities and flavor and, in this way, attaining mastery in the depths of one's heart. What one does thereafter will attain the realm of "cold" and "emaciated" and give pleasure. However, those who are by no means able to afford fine utensils should not concern themselves with obtaining them. The important thing is to recognize good quality in wherever one finds it.

Self-importance and egotism are obstructions. Yet the art cannot be mastered without self-esteem. A dictum states: "Become the master of your heart, but do not let your heart master you"— the words of an ancient.[21]

Perhaps in order to enhance Murata Shukō's prestige, Yamanoue Sōji stated that Shukō had been in the service of Yoshimasa. A *kakemono* in Yoshimasa's handwriting with a dedication to Shukō indicates that Shukō and Yoshimasa must have been personally acquainted. Kumakura believed, however, that their acquaintance was not direct and that Nōami served as an intermediary between the two men. Be that as it may, it is likely that if Yoshimasa was so impressed by Shukō's opinions about tea that he sent him a painting, it also is likely that he was influenced by him. Modern critics who accept this view believe that Yoshimasa should be ranked alongside Shukō as the originator of *wabicha*.[22]

The similarity between *renga* and *chanoyu* existed on another level. Both arts required more than one participant. A *waka* might be composed in the privacy of the poet's room or in a lonely retreat, but a *renga* sequence was generally the joint composition of a group of people who shared the pleasure of poetic composition. Tea could, of course, be consumed in solitude, but *chanoyu* usually required guests to drink tea together, enjoying not only the fragrance of the tea and the feel of the tea bowl in their hands but also the simple but highly refined architecture of the *chashitsu*, the *tokonoma* with its single flower in an unobtrusive vase, the scroll in the hand of a Zen master, and, above all, the pleasure that came from sharing the experience with like-minded people. Both *renga* and tea were appropriate arts for a world wasted by endless warfare. Outside the room where friends drank tea or composed *renga* together, there might be battle cries and the desolation of a city ravaged by warfare and neglect, but inside there was the warmth of human companionship.

The rules that govern each step in the preparation and consumption of the tea may seem unnecessary complications to what is, after all, no more than a simple matter of drinking tea. But the elevation of tea drinking to the special level of ritual, in a manner that drinking saké (let alone beer) never achieved, directly and indirectly affected many arts.

Chanoyu has largely been responsible for the amazing development of ceramics, the art in which Japan dominates the world. When the Portuguese first came to Japan in the late sixteenth century, they were impressed by the cleanliness of the houses and the way that meals were served, but they expressed bafflement that simple bowls, even those devoid of ornamentation and not rimmed in gold like European bowls, fetched enormous sums. One priest wrote about *chanoyu* as performed in a *chashitsu*:

> Because they greatly value and enjoy this kind of gathering to drink tea, they spend large sums of money in building such a house, rough though it may be, and in purchasing the things needed for drinking the kind of tea which is offered in these meet-

ings. Thus there are utensils, albeit of earthenware, which come to be worth ten, twenty or thirty thousand *crusados* or even more—a thing which will appear as madness and barbarity to other nations that know of it.[23]

Today *chanoyu* supports hundreds, if not thousands, of potters. If it did not exist, the demand for artistic pottery would be about what it is in the West: restricted to the relatively small number of connoisseurs who prize bowls or vases for their shape and color, without considering their possible use. But thanks to *chanoyu*, there is a steady demand for tea bowls, jugs, vases, plates, and the like. Tea bowls are often extremely expensive, though to an outsider they do not seem to be especially difficult to make. Their price is high, we are told, because the potter puts his soul into them. It may be because they possess something of the potter's soul that they are given names as if they were living things.

Unlike *renga*, *chanoyu* is very much a part of Japanese culture today, but like so much else that is known as part of the "soul of Japan," it was born in the brief interlude between the wars when Yoshimasa resided at the Ginkaku-ji.

10

Yoshimasa's interests extended to every art practiced in his time. In some he ranked as a central figure, but he was a devotee also of arts with which his name is not often associated, such as perfume blending (kōdō).[1] He studied with distinguished teachers and became proficient in each art, though not necessarily a master. There is no way now to rate his skill in performing the tea ceremony or in blending perfumes, but his surviving poetry, both *waka* and *renga*, displays a high level of competence.[2] But even more than his own achievements, his encouragement of the arts earns him an important place in cultural history.

The arts, however, were by no means Yoshimasa's sole interest; he also was deeply religious throughout his life.[3] Yoshimasa's closest ties, as we have seen, were with Zen Buddhism, the sect favored by the samurai class. From his childhood, Yoshimasa associated with Zen monks, and he seems to have found the practice of Zen particularly congenial when applying himself to the arts. He was not interested in studying the sutras or pondering religious principles but believed that Buddhist enlightenment could be experienced in any activity. The following *waka* may reveal his basic Zen outlook:

kotonoha no	The path of the law
hoka ni idetaru	Which exists quite apart from
nori no michi	Verbal expression—
tare ni ka towan	Whom can one ask about it?
tare ka kotaen	Who will answer one's questions?[4]

After Yoshimasa abdicated as shogun and withdrew from political and military activity, he entered orders as a Zen monk. He had always been a generous protector of Zen temples, so it was natural for him to choose Zen when he decided to "abandon the world," if only because it had been the Buddhism favored by earlier Ashikaga shoguns. Although he kept works of Zen philosophy by his side, his devotion to Zen did not stem from any deep understanding of its teachings. Even after a lifetime of exposure to Zen doctrines, he apparently possessed only an elementary acquaintance with its essential teachings and history.[5] Rather, to Yoshimasa, the chief appeal of Zen lay in its outer manifestations; he found in the severe simplicity of Zen worship something of the beauty he sought in the arts that most appealed to him: architecture, gardens, flower arrangement, the tea ceremony, and nō.

Yoshimasa's religious life was by no means, however, restricted to Zen. A special trust in the bodhisattva Kannon that went back to his early twenties remained with him to the end of his life. Furthermore, the Silver Pavilion was built primarily as a place where he might worship Kannon, a clear indication that he never lost this faith.

In addition to Kannon, Yoshimasa paid special homage to Amida Buddha. A belief in the saving grace of Amida was shared by many members of the aristocracy who came to doubt that the performance of good works would bring them salvation, as earlier Buddhist sects had preached. In times of warfare and other disasters, good works—the temples they built, the sutras they had copied, and the like—were so easily destroyed that they seemed unlikely to ensure lasting benefits. Although Zen monks believed that salvation could be gained by quietly sitting and cultivating the Buddhahood within oneself, there were many hindrances to quiet meditation in the turbulent times. Therefore, many people, despairing of the possibility of gaining salvation by their own efforts (*jiriki*), turned to Amida Buddha, relying on his strength (*tariki*) to save all men, as he had vowed.

Ōjō yōshū (*Essentials of Salvation*), a work written by the monk Genshin (942–1017) with the purpose of helping others discover the means of gaining salvation, opens with a description of the conditions in which people of his time found themselves:

The teaching and practice which leads to birth in Paradise is the most important thing in this impure world during these degenerate times. Monks and laymen, men of high or low station, who will not turn to it? But the literature of the exoteric and esoteric teachings of Buddha are not one in text, and the practices of one's work in this life in its ritualistic and philosophic aspects are many. They are not difficult for men of keen wisdom and great diligence, but how can a stupid person such as I achieve this knowledge? Because of this I have chosen the one gate of the *nembutsu* to salvation.[6]

Genshin modestly called himself "stupid." He definitely was not stupid, but it was probably difficult even for learned and diligent monks to understand fully the voluminous writings of the different sects of Buddhism. Reciting the *nenbutsu*, the plea for salvation addressed to Amida Buddha, offered the best hope of rebirth in the Pure Land.

If this was true of Genshin's time, it was even more applicable to Yoshimasa's. The meaningless destruction during the Ōnin War demonstrated how right Genshin had been to characterize the world as "impure." Many people, both those at the court who led privileged lives and those on farms or on fishing boats who were too badly educated to understand even the simplest Buddhist teachings, desperately wanted to be saved, and they turned to the *nenbutsu*, the one sure gate to salvation.

The importance of reciting the invocation to Amida Buddha was successively preached by Hōnen, Shinran, Ippen, and other celebrated priests of Jōdo (Pure Land) Buddhism, each further simplifying the means until salvation was within the grasp of even the least educated person. Hōnen insisted that it was essential to address the invocation to Amida repeatedly, day and night, in order to demonstrate how completely one had placed one's faith in Amida's mercy. Shinran, however, declared that salvation was not a reward granted for having recited the *nenbutsu*. Rather, it came as a gift from Amida Buddha, in keeping with his original vow. Ippen had a vision that not even faith in Amida was necessary for salvation; all that was needed to be reborn in the Pure Land was a single invocation of the *nenbutsu*, which did not even have to be said aloud but merely thought.

A further development in Pure Land Buddhism came with Rennyo (1415–1499), a contemporary of Yoshimasa, who believed that the *nenbutsu* should not be considered a prayer addressed to Amida Buddha asking to be saved, but an expression of gratitude for Amida's gift of salvation, which was granted regardless of a person's faults and whether or not the person had achieved merit.[7] Through his easy-to-understand versions of Shinran's teachings, known as *ofumi*, Rennyo was able to establish Jōdo shinshū as by far the most popular sect of Buddhism in Japan. He also rebuilt the Hongan-ji, the great central temple of Pure Land Buddhism, which earlier had been destroyed by priests from the Tendai monastery on Mount Hiei.

Although Rennyo was the leading Buddhist figure of the day, he seems not to have influenced Yoshimasa. In part this was because during most of his life, Rennyo's proselytization activities took place away from the capital, but the main reason was probably that Rennyo's Buddhism was intended for and had the greatest appeal to the lower classes. In contrast, Yoshimasa's Jōdo Buddhism, in the traditions of Hōnen rather than Shinran or Rennyo, still involved ritual observances of a kind congenial to members of the court.

Numerous records attest to the frequency of Yoshimasa's visits to Jōdo temples. For example, in 1474 he (along with his wife, Hino Tomiko, and his son Yoshihisa) visited Seigan-ji, a temple associated with Hōnen, and in the following year the three visited Konkō-ji, famous for its "dancing" *nenbutsu*. In 1484 Yoshimasa went to the Chion'in, where he offered incense and devoutly worshiped the portrait of Hōnen, the founder of the temple. On several occasions, he visited Shinnyo-dō, another temple closely associated with Hōnen, and after the Ōnin War he gave money for the reconstruction of this temple. Yoshimasa's devotion to Amida Buddha in his late years may initially have been inspired by the popularity of Jōdo Buddhism at the court, where he attended sermons and discussions of *Essentials of Salvation*. But even if his interest in Jōdo Buddhism was first stimulated by a desire to share the beliefs preferred by the nobility, it eventually became his deepest religious conviction.

Amida's promise of salvation brought Yoshimasa greater comfort than did the austere Zen teachings he otherwise admired. Although his public and aesthetic life owed much to Zen, in his private life Yoshimasa depended increasingly on the *nenbutsu*. His combination of *jiriki* and *tariki* Buddhism was by no means unusual at this time, when every possible aid to salvation was eagerly sought.

Particularly while he was shogun, Yoshimasa also visited temples belonging to the older sects of Buddhism, especially the Shingon and Tendai temples in Kyoto and the Kōfuku-ji in Nara. When some member of his family was ill, he quite naturally summoned priests of Esoteric Buddhism to chant spells for the person's recovery. He probably felt no contradiction that a believer in Zen and Jōdo Buddhism should ask the help of these priests. Regardless of the variety of Buddhism followed by the spell-working priests, they were specialists in praying for the recovery of people suffering from illness, and their prayers were more likely to be efficacious than those of priests with other skills. Similarly, Yoshimasa often turned for help to practitioners of yin-yang divination and to astrologers, believing that their special knowledge, though not based on Buddhism, could also preserve him from misfortune. He was glad to receive whatever help was available to save him from the evil that abounded in an impure world.

Yoshimasa's advisers included priests who belonged to different sects, and they seem to have associated peaceably, even though violence between sects or even between members of the same sect was not uncommon. There were frequent incidents when, for example, the monks of some temple, jealous of its privileges, decided to attack a rival temple of the same sect that they thought was infringing on these privileges. Violence was less likely to arise from doctrinal differences than from disputes over property, but religious factionalism also could be a problem. The most conspicuous instances of violence carried out by believers of one Buddhist sect against members of other sects were the *ikkō ikki* uprisings staged by followers of Rennyo in the Hokuriku region. Deploring these excesses of devotion to his school, in 1473 Rennyo issued a set of eleven rules (*okite*) that members of his school were to obey. The second and third implicitly condemned the uprisings:

Never slander the various teachings of the various schools.

Do not attack other schools by comparing them to the practices of our own school.[8]

Yoshimasa, paying little attention to these disputes, worshiped not only at many Buddhist temples, regardless of their affiliation, but also at Shinto shrines, especially while he was shogun. He always manifested a devout belief in the Shinto gods: in times of natural disasters—drought, floods, epidemics, and the like—or when warfare raged, his prayers were offered first of all to the gods. He seems to have believed that because Japan was the land of the gods, the gods would grant the Japanese special protection in times of adversity, provided that he, the shogun, offered his prayers to them. After Yoshimasa resigned as shogun, his visits to Shinto shrines became less frequent, suggesting that he prayed to the gods mainly in his capacity as shogun rather than because of personal religious devotion.

As we have seen, the last years of Yoshimasa's life were devoted largely to the planning and construction of the Higashiyama mountain retreat. Some of the buildings were intended as both living quarters for Yoshimasa and places where he might entertain friends, but most of the buildings were for his private use in worship. The Tōgu-dō, originally called the Amida-dono, enshrined Yoshimasa's *jibutsu* (personal Buddha), a statue of Amida, and the *fusuma* paintings depicted persons important in Jōdo scriptures. (The building was modified when it became a Zen temple after Yoshimasa's death.)

Among the secular activities at the Higashiyama retreat were performances of nō, perhaps staged in conjunction with religious observances. Nō may have been the art to which Yoshimasa was most devoted. He was only eight years old when Zeami, the supreme master of nō, died in 1443, but two other important nō actors were active during his maturity: Konparu Zenchiku (1405–1480) and Kanze On'ami (1399–1467).

Zenchiku was not only an outstanding performer but also second only to Zeami as a playwright and theorist of the art of nō. His best-known work of criticism, *Rokurin ichiro* (*Six Circles, One Dewdrop*), is an abstruse work that embodies his philosophical and religious interpretation of the effects of nō performances. Arthur H. Thornhill described the work as follows:

> Devised to represent a host of aesthetic, dramaturgical, and pedagogical principles Zenchiku received in training from his teacher Zeami, this symbolic topology of seven categories can be seen as a repository of Zeami's teachings. . . . The six circles are analyzed as embodying a "centrifugal" progression, which delineates the generation of specific artistic effects, and also a "centripetal" process, by which the actor develops even more profound levels of his art.[9]

Zenchiku received extensive personal instruction from Zeami, even though they belonged to different schools. (Zenchiku belonged to the Konparu school.) Recognizing the younger man's unusual talent, Zeami composed two treatises, "Six Principles" (Rikugi) and "Finding Gems and Gaining the Flower" (Shūgyoku tokka), for Zenchiku's benefit.[10] "Finding Gems and Gaining the Flower" contains principles that appear in *Six Circles, One Dewdrop*.

Unfortunately for Zenchiku, Zeami much earlier had designated Motoshige (better known as On'ami) as his successor.[11] In 1399, at the age of thirty-six or thirty-seven, Zeami, despairing of having a son, decided to adopt as his heir the infant son of his younger brother. The child, at first known as Saburō (and later as Motoshige),[12] received from Zeami the induction into the art of nō that Zeami himself had received from his father, Kan'ami. However, a year or two after Zeami adopted Saburō, his own wife gave birth to a son, who was known as Motomasa.[13] She later gave birth to another son, Motoyoshi, and a daughter. Inevitably, rivalry grew up between the adopted son and the two biological sons, but while the three boys were still young, Zeami taught them impartially.

Although appreciative of Zenchiku's talents, Zeami did not believe that he was as yet qualified to succeed him. In the meantime, Zeami became increasingly aware of Motomasa's extraordinary talents. He wrote that Motomasa was even superior to Kan'ami, amazing praise considering that Zeami considered his father to be in every respect the supreme artist of nō.[14] Accordingly, Zeami gave his "Teachings on Style and the Flower" (Fūshi kaden) not to Motoshige, officially his eldest son, but to Motomasa. The reason he gave these secret writings to Motomasa and no one else was that in keeping with the esoteric traditions of transmitting knowledge, he believed that only the most worthy son should be permitted to learn the secrets of the art.[15] Zeami obviously hoped that Motomasa would be his successor, but he died prematurely, to Zeami's profound sorrow.

With the death of Motomasa, who had written several superb nō, Zenchiku became the heir to Zeami's traditions. Zenchiku's plays include some of the most poignant in the nō repertory: *Bashō*, *Yōkihi*, *Teika*, and *Nonomiya*.[16] It has been said of them that they "consistently embody the neoclassical aesthetic ideal of yūgen, radiating a wistful sadness and nostalgia for the past brilliance and elegance of court culture. The art of poetry is a major theme, reflecting Zenchiku's stated view that waka is the essence of sarugaku."[17]

Yoshimasa certainly saw Zenchiku perform,[18] but (like Ashikaga Yoshinori), he apparently preferred On'ami. It is difficult to appraise On'ami today because, an exception among the major figures in the art of nō, he did not leave any plays or works of nō criticism. We also lack objective contemporary evaluations of his skill as an actor, but there is reason to suppose that his style of acting was more dynamic than that of Zeami or Zenchiku. His realism excited audiences because it underlined the drama in the play's events. Zenchiku, in contrast, did not try to excite audiences with dramatic effects but instead move them more profoundly with abstract, symbolic beauty.

On'ami had been a favorite of Yoshinori even before the latter renounced his calling as a Buddhist priest. Once he became the shogun, Yoshinori's admiration for On'ami led him to assume the role of a patron, and when On'ami broke away from the mainstream of the Kanze-za to form a separate group, Yoshinori openly preferred his performances to those of Zeami or Zenchiku. The split seems to have been caused by On'ami's resentment that although he was officially the heir to Zeami's position as head of the *za* (troupe), Zeami continued to display favoritism toward his son Motomasa. It may be that Zeami himself engineered the split, hoping that if On'ami were affiliated with a separate branch, he would not attempt to become his successor as head of the Kanze troupe.[19]

After Yoshinori became shogun in 1428, his preference for On'ami became even more conspicuous. He made no secret of this preference: On'ami regularly performed not only in the shogun's palace but also in the palace of the cloistered emperor (*sendō*). Performances by Zeami's troupe, in contrast, were few and far between. In effect, the splinter Kanze group became the main Kanze troupe, with Kanze On'ami Motoshige as its head.

On'ami's reputation has suffered over the years because of his association with Ashikaga Yoshinori's decision to send Zeami into exile on Sado Island. We really do not know the direct cause of Zeami's exile at the age of seventy-two.[20] It has often been said that it was because Zeami had refused Yoshinori's command to turn over to On'ami the secrets of his school. But in view of Yoshinori's reputation as an unusually bloodthirsty tyrant, it hardly seems likely that Zeami (or anyone else) would have refused to obey his command. Perhaps something Zeami did, something of no intrinsic significance, irritated Yoshinori, and that was sufficient reason to send him into exile. While Zeami was in exile on Sado, On'ami's troupe flourished. It had come to be considered the main Kanze school.

The death of Yoshinori, murdered while watching a performance of nō, undoubtedly came as a blow to On'ami, but he was not discouraged. Even though he no longer had the special protection of the shogun, he continued to stage subscription performances (*kanjin nō*) in many parts of the country and enjoyed a unique popularity. Without question, On'ami was a highly accomplished performer, which may be why he was offered the patronage of the new shogun, Yoshimasa. In times of constant disorder, most nō actors had trouble maintaining their art, and even the Kanze school was so impoverished that Yoshimasa ordered several daimyos to contribute money for the troupe. On'ami, however, continued to thrive despite generally adverse conditions and remained popular, especially among the common people.

Yoshimasa gave On'ami his undivided support. He proclaimed the Kanze troupe (On'ami's branch) to be "the nō of the shogun's family" (*shōgun-ke no sarugaku*), and he was directly responsible for establishing Kanze as the highest ranking of the four schools of nō.[21] In the fourth month of 1464, subscription performances of nō were staged over a period of three days at Tadasugawara, one of the most brilliant occasions in nō's entire history. The actors were headed by Matasaburō, On'ami's son, who himself now enjoyed Yoshimasa's protection. Even though On'ami was now in his sixty-seventh year, he took an important part, appearing in more than ten plays. He continued to perform until his death three years later. On'ami had established himself as Zeami's successor not because he had been adopted by Zeami but because of his own surpassing skill. Dōmoto Masaki believes that surviving documents make it clear that as a performer, On'ami was superior even to Zeami.

Both Yoshimitsu and Yoshinori patronized nō actors, but it was Yoshimasa who established nō as the "music" of the state. According to Confucian tradition, "rites and music" (*reigaku*) were an indispensable part of any well-ordered state. Rites maintained order, and music exercised a good influence on people's emotions. Yoshimasa's appreciation of nō certainly was not confined to its beneficial effects. He found in the nō the mystery and depth associated with the word *yūgen*, an evocation of a world beyond the visible one.

The oldest surviving nō robes date from Yoshimasa's time and may have been woven for him, as their sober but elegant taste suggests. A jacket (*happi*) of dark green material woven with gold thread in designs of paired dragonflies, owned by the Kanze family, is in typically unassertive taste. One can imagine Yoshimasa, after a particularly brilliant performance of nō, removing his jacket and offering it to the principal actor, rather as a Spaniard throws an article of clothing into a bull ring by way of homage to a superlative matador. The presentation of robes as a reward for an excellent performance goes back as far as Zeami's day.[22]

The patronage of nō was continued by the Tokugawa shoguns, who believed themselves to be the heirs of the Ashikaga shoguns. They treated nō as the official music of the state, believing that if they recognized the importance of the Confucian principle of rites and music, it would contribute to the peace and security of their reigns. But regardless of their reasons, they helped perpetuate a noble art.

In each of the arts, Yoshimasa's patronage was essential to its development. The Higashiyama era was a brilliant period in cultural history, and its effects extended far beyond the seven years that it lasted. The guiding spirit throughout, it goes without saying, was Yoshimasa himself, as his taste was reflected in all the arts of the era.

Yoshimasa's happy life during his last years was shadowed by palsy, which first became noticeable in 1485. Depression accompanied the palsy, but Yoshimasa was comforted by the pleasures of the mountain retreat and heartened by the new seriousness of his son Yoshihisa, whose display of prowess on the battlefield against enemies of the shogunate promised a return to the days of the Ashikaga glory. This made the news of Yoshihisa's death during the fighting in Ōmi Province an even greater shock to Yoshimasa.

On May 22, 1489, the night after funeral services were conducted for Yoshihisa, Yoshimasa suffered a severe attack of palsy that paralyzed his left side. At this point, he had to consider who should be the next shogun, for now that Yoshihisa was dead, there was no obvious choice. Yoshimi, whom Yoshimasa had at one time named as his successor, was disqualified because he had served as the chief of the Western Army during the latter part of the Ōnin War,[23] and Yoshimi's son, Yoshitane, was suspect for the same reason. Yoshimasa thus felt that despite his illness, he had no choice but to resume the post of shogun. Construction was begun on a building at the retreat where he might conduct official business, but the palsy afflicting Yoshimasa grew noticeably worse. The deterioration of his health was blamed on the direction faced by the new building, so it was torn down, but Yoshimasa's health did not improve.

Late in 1489, Yoshimi and Yoshitane visited Yoshimasa at the retreat. Yoshimi had once more put on Buddhist robes, a sign that he had abandoned any thought of becoming the shogun. Impressed by this resolution, Yoshimasa adopted Yoshitane as his successor. A month later, Yoshimasa grew sicker. He fell into a coma and died on January 28, 1490. Yoshitane became the new shogun.

During his last years, Yoshimasa's relations with his wife, Hino Tomiko, improved. He may have been impressed by the vast amount of money she gave for the funeral expenses of their son Yoshihisa. They continued, however, to live apart, and it is not clear whether she attended Yoshimasa's funeral. His grave is in the Shōkoku-ji, a temple whose history mirrored the rise and fall of the Ashikaga shoguns.

The Higashiyama culture thrived in the island of relative calm between the end of the Ōnin War and the beginning of the wars of the sixteenth century. Its duration was brief and the participants were not numerous, but its effects on later Japanese culture were immense. Much of what Japanese think of today as being especially Japanese, especially close to every Japanese, even though modernization and globalization have affected the lives of all in Japan, can be traced back to this period.

Yoshimasa may have been the worst shogun ever to rule Japan. He was a total failure as a soldier. During his reign as shogun, the shogunate grew progressively weaker. Yoshimasa was no more successful in his private life. But in terms of the cultural developments that took place while Yoshimasa lived in Higashiyama, he was by no means a failure. We may even be tempted to conclude that no man in the history of Japan had a greater influence on the formation of Japanese taste. This was his sole, but very important, redeeming feature. The worst of the shoguns was the best, the only one to leave a lasting heritage for the entire Japanese people.

Introduction

1. For a detailed and persuasive account of Yoshi-mitsu's relations with the throne, see Imatani Akira, *Nihon kokuō to domin*, pp. 39–56.

2. The term *shugo* is often translated as "constable." This translation is appropriate for the Kamakura period, but when writing about the Muromachi period, John W. Hall and Jeffrey P. Mass explain the term *shugo* as a "provincial military governor, appointed by the Muromachi *bakufu*" (*Medieval Japan: Essays in Institutional History*, p. 259).

3. Hayashiya Tatsusaburō, "Kyoto in the Muromachi Age," in *Japan in the Muromachi Age*, ed. John Whitney Hall and Toyoda Takeshi, p. 22. Yoshimasa's letter was in response to a message from Yoshihisa urging Yoshimasa not to remove himself excessively

from worldly affairs. Yoshimasa had expressed identical sentiments in a letter dated 1476.

4. There also is a statue of Tokugawa Ieyasu, the first shogun of the Tokugawa line, suggesting that an attempt had been made to link the Ashikaga and Tokugawa families, both of which traced their ancestry to the Minamoto clan.

5. For a description of these short stories, known familiarly as *otogi-zōshi* (companion library), see Donald Keene, *Seeds in the Heart*, pp. 1092–1119.

6. Quoted in Keene, *Seeds in the Heart*, pp. 942–43. See also Steven D. Carter, *Regent Redux*, pp. 145–47.

7. See the interesting study of the "renaissance" by Nishida Masayoshi, *Nihon no runessansu.*

Chapter 1

1. Imatani Akira, *Ashikaga shōgun ansatsu*, p. 86. Gosukō-in, the father of Emperor Go-Hanazono, was the author of *Kanmon gyoki* (*Record of Things Heard and Seen*), a diary covering the years 1416 to 1448. The diary is a major source of information on the political and cultural life of the time.

2. Imatani Akira, *Nihon kokuō to domin*, pp. 92–93. Imatani stresses the importance of Yoshimochi's insistence on abiding by the decision of the senior retainers, contrasting this policy with the absolute rule typical of earlier shoguns. See also Tanaka Yoshinari, *Ashikaga jidai shi*, pp. 131–32.

3. Gien was Yoshinori's Buddhist name. He ranked as a *junsangō*, meaning that he came in precedence next after the "three empresses": the grand dowager empress, the dowager empress, and the reigning empress. This was a conventional term and did not imply that all three empresses were still alive.

   This account, taken from Imatani (*Nihon kokuō*, pp. 94–95), differs from that given by the nobleman Madenokōji Tokifusa, according to which Mitsuie three times drew lots before the altar of the Iwashimizu Shrine, and each time the slip with Yoshimochi's name appeared. See Steven D. Carter, *Regent Redux*, p. 29.

4. Imatani, *Nihon kokuō*, pp. 94–96. Tanaka warns against accepting uncritically the account of the lottery given in contemporary diaries (*Ashikaga jidai shi*, p. 133); rather, he seems to think that the lottery was rigged.

5. For the diary entry, see Imatani, *Nihon kokuō*, p. 107.

6. Imatani, *Ashikaga shōgun ansatsu*, pp. 57–58.

7. Ibid., p. 59. See also Nagahara Keiji, *Gekokujō no jidai*, pp. 53–54.

8. Tanaka, *Ashikaga jidai shi*, pp. 150–55. For details of the circumstances under which Yoshinori got rid of Isshiki Yoshitsura, see Carter, *Regent Redux*, pp. 64–65. Tanaka also describes Yoshinori's similar punishment of another daimyo, Toki Mochiyori. See also Imatani, *Nihon kokuō*, p. 111. Although characterizing Yoshinori in terms of "The Shogun as Autocrat" (*Japan's Renaissance: The Politics of the Muromachi Bakufu*, p. 43) and not hesitating to admit that "when unstable tenures did not accomplish his objectives, murder served him equally well" (p. 45), Kenneth Alan Grossberg paints a generally favorable portrait of Yoshinori. He concludes his evaluation of Yoshinori in these terms: "He bequeathed the mixed blessing of a growing economy, a tradition of shogunal artistic patronage worthy of a Renaissance prince, and an overwhelming political turmoil which his inexperienced successor was hard put to set to rights" (p. 52). Grossberg does not, however, hint at the reign of terror initiated by Yoshinori, perhaps considering his cruelty no more than what one would expect of a Renaissance tyrant.

9. No doubt robbers and other criminals were executed for misdeeds, but their punishment does not figure in the diaries of the time.

10. Imatani, *Ashikaga shōgun ansatsu*, p. 86. *Kennaiki*, the diary kept by Tokifusa from 1414 to 1455, is an important source of information about this period.

11. This was one of sixty-six temples of the same name established by Ashikaga Takauji after his triumph over the forces of Emperor Go-Daigo. The name means "bring peace to the country," and it was expected that people would pray at these temples that the country would enjoy peace.

12. *Kakitsu monogatari*, Zoku gunsho ruijū series, *kan* 577, p. 228. Although as the word *monogatari* indicates, this is not a work of

history and the text is literarily decorated, much can be verified from historical sources. See Imatani, *Ashikaga shōgun ansatsu*, p. 211. The three provinces controlled by the Akamatsu family were Harima, Bizen, and Mimasaka.

13. *Kakitsu monogatari*, p. 231.
14. Imatani, *Ashikaga shōgun ansatsu*, pp. 100–101. Imatani, quoting Mitsusuke's letter from the war tale *Akamatsu jōsui ki*, states that even though the historicity of this war tale as a whole has been authenticated in recent years, he had some doubts about the letter.
15. Imatani, *Ashikaga shōgun ansatsu*, p. 102.
16. Mochitoyo is generally known by his Buddhist name, Yamana Sōzen.
17. Quoted in Imatani, *Ashikaga shōgun ansatsu*, p. 106.
18. Ibid., p. 108. The edict, dated the first day of the eighth month and signed by the court official Bōjō Toshihide, was addressed to Hosokawa Mochiyuki, the shogunal deputy.

Chapter 2

1. Imatani Akira, *Ashikaga shōgun ansatsu*, p. 155.
2. Nagahara Keiji, *Gekokujō no jidai*, p. 80; Imatani, *Ashikaga shōgun ansatsu*, p. 136.
3. For the *tokusei*, see Imatani, *Ashikaga shōgun ansatsu*, p. 114. It is not clear from the text what specifically induced the manor lords (*satanin*) to issue it.
4. The Hokke-dō (now called the Honkoku-ji), a major temple of the Nichiren sect, was burned down along with a section of the Shimo-kyō area. See Imatani, *Ashikaga shōgun ansatsu*, p. 141.
5. Quoted in Imatani, *Ashikaga shōgun ansatsu*, p. 144.
6. For the *tokusei*, issued on the eighteenth day of the ninth intercalary month, see Imatani, *Ashikaga shōgun ansatsu*, pp. 189–90.
7. H. Paul Varley, *The Ōnin War*, p. 78.
8. Some scholars believe that Yoshikatsu's death was occasioned by a fall from a horse. As a samurai boy, he doubtless was encouraged to ride even before he was old enough to control a horse, but there is no firm evidence that a fall was the cause of his death. See Kawai Masaharu, *Ashikaga Yoshimasa*, p. 25.

9. I have called him by a name that he did not assume until 1453, when he was seventeen. His boyhood name was Miharu. When he was ten, his name was changed to Yoshishige. Both characters used to write this name contain the element *hoko*, meaning "spear." Although it was quite a good name for a military man, the spears did not suit a peace-loving shogun, who therefore changed his name to the nonbelligerent Yoshimasa.

10. Kawai, *Ashikaga Yoshimasa*, p. 33.

11. Although Ashikaga Yoshimitsu had unified the country in 1392, ending the division into two courts (the Northern Court in Kyoto and the Southern Court in Yoshino), there still were bands of men loyal to the latter who made sporadic attacks.

12. Yoshimasa did not actually become shogun until 1449, but he was the shogun-designate.

13. The family had taken the surname Hino from the district south of Kyoto where Hino Sukenari built the Yakushi Hall of the Hōkai-ji in the eleventh century. The family was also known as Uramatsu. See Morita Kyōji, *Ashikaga Yoshimasa no kenkyū*, p. 25.

14. Although this lady is always referred to as Imamairi or Oimamairi, this was not her real name but a general term for a woman recently arrived at the court.

15. For a detailed account of Hino Shigeko's meddling, see Takahashi Osamu, "Hino (Uramatsu) Shigeko ni kansuru ikkōsatsu," *Kokushigaku*, no. 137.

16. For more on Yoshimasa's calligraphy, see Matsubara Shigeru, ed., *Muromachi: Ashikaga Yoshimasa hyakushu waka*, pp. 64–65.

17. Morita, *Ashikaga Yoshimasa*, p. 27.

18. Ibid., p. 55. Morita's source was *Gaun nikkenroku*, the diary of Zuikei Shūhō, a priest of the Shōkoku-ji. Oima was, of course, Imamairi. Arima Mochiie, a member of the Akamatsu family, was disliked for his efforts to ingratiate himself with the court. Karasumaru Suketō, called Karasuma (as in Kyoto today), was a member of the Hino family and had maintained close connections with Yoshimasa from his childhood.

19. Yoshimura Teiji, *Hino Tomiko*, p. 38.

20. According to Kawai, Tomiko gave birth to a son (*Ashikaga Yoshimasa*, p. 37); however, Yoshimura says that the child was a girl (*Hino Tomiko*, p. 44). Morita evades the issue by saying that Tomiko gave birth to a baby (*sekishi*) (*Ashikaga Yoshimasa*, p. 57).

21. Kawai, *Ashikaga Yoshimasa*, p. 37. See also Morita, *Ashikaga Yoshimasa*, p. 57.

22. Kuwata Tadachika, ed., *Ashikaga shōgun retsuden*, pp. 200–201. The son, Gihaku, became the imperial priest (*monzeki*) at the Sanbōin, but I have been unable to discover more about him.

23. Morita, *Ashikaga Yoshimasa*, pp. 58–59. He quotes *Daijōin jisha zōjiki*, the diary of Jinson (1430–1508), the abbot of the Daijō-in, a subtemple of the Kōfuku-ji in Nara. Jinson was a son of Ichijō Kaneyoshi. The diary entry for the twenty-ninth day of the seventh month of Bunmei 9 (1477) relates how Sōgi, visiting Nara from the capital, had brought the latest news. See Suzuki Ryōichi, *Daijōin jisha zōjiki*, p. 201.

24. Yoshimura, *Hino Tomiko*, p. 115.

25. Ikkyū used the poetic name Fusō for Japan. This rather free rendering of the poem follows the interpretation in Hirano Sōjō, *Kyōunshū zenshaku*, vol. 1, pp. 259–60.

26. Hirano, *Kyōunshū zenshaku*, vol. 1, p. 260. "Smoke and dust" suggests battlefields. The "east wind" may be the Hosokawa forces who brought temporary relief from the east. Yang Kuei-fei was killed at Ma-wei. Hirano believed that these poems were written about 1474 when the Ōnin War had subsided and Tomiko had assumed the powers of the shogun.

Chapter 3

1. Yokoi Kiyoshi, *Higashiyama bunka*, pp. 110–20.

2. The term "seven entrances" (*shichikō*) was frequently used, but the number was not exact; "seven" stood for all the roads into Kyoto, regardless of the actual number. See Yokoi, *Higashiyama bunka*, p. 117.

3. Yokoi, *Higashiyama bunka*, p. 119. The monk was Tōgen Zuisen (1430–1489), known for his commentaries on Chinese classical texts.

4. Morita Kyōji, *Ashikaga Yoshimasa no kenkyū*, pp. 75–76. Morita refutes the long-standing belief that Yoshimasa was totally indifferent to the hardships suffered by the people at this time, citing the money Yoshimasa gave to relieve poverty and the houses he built to shelter those who had been left destitute by the famine. These acts of generosity, mainly performed by subordinates, did not necessarily originate with Yoshimasa, but he clearly was not indifferent to suffering.

5. Yokoi, *Higashiyama bunka*, pp. 120–21. The dream is said to have occurred on the eighteenth day of the first month.

6. The story is in *Inryōken nichiroku*, the diary of the priest Kikei Shinzui (1401–1469), cited in Kawai Masaharu, *Ashikaga Yoshimasa*, p. 42.

7. Unsen Taikyoku, *Hekizan nichiroku*, ed. Takeuchi Rizō, p. 74. There is another translation of this passage in H. Paul Varley, *The Ōnin War*, p. 117. A similar entry, describing the behavior of nobles on an excursion to see the plum blossoms, is dated the eighteenth day of the second month of 1461 (p. 110).

8. Shimura Kunihiro, *Ōnin ki*, pp. 252–53, in Varley, *Ōnin War*, p. 140.

9. Taikyoku, *Hekizan nichiroku*, p. 112. The entry is dated the third day of the third month of 1461.

10. Mount Shou-yang is where Po-i, who hated the Chou dynasty, lived on fern shoots (and eventually starved) rather than serve the Chou. See Burton Watson, trans., *Records of the Grand Historian of China*, vol. 2, p. 453.

11. *(Shinsen) Chōroku kanshō ki*, p. 237, a chronicle by an unknown scribe that covers the period from 1460 to 1465, quoted in Kawai, *Ashikaga Yoshimasa*, p. 45; and Yokoi, *Higashiyama bunka*, p. 125.

12. Ibid. The "lord" in the poem is the emperor, and the "vassal" is the shogun. Haga Kōshirō has expressed the belief that the story of the emperor composing a poem of reproach was probably true (*Higashiyama bunka*, p. 16), but other scholars have disagreed.

13. Yokoi, *Higashiyama bunka*, p. 126.

14. Shimura, *Ōnin ki*, p. 254, in Varley, *Ōnin War*, p. 143.

15. Morita, *Ashikaga Yoshimasa*, p. 82. Yoshimi was known as Imadegawa-dono, from the site of his palace, which originally belonged to the Sanjō, his mother's family.

16. There were rumors that the father of the child was not Yoshimasa but Emperor Go-Hanazono. See Yoshimura Teiji, *Hino Tomiko*, pp. 71–72. The rumors, first reported in *Ōnin kōki*, were convincingly refuted in Sasakawa Tanerō, *Higashiyama jidai no bunka*, pp. 67–68.

17. Shimura, *Ōnin ki*, pp. 154–55, in Varley, *Ōnin War*, pp. 144–45.

18. Shimura, *Ōnin ki*, p. 252, in Varley, *Ōnin War*, p. 139. Tomiko and Shigeko are in the original *midaidokoro* and Kōju-in.

19. Murasaki Shikibu, *The Tale of Genji*, trans. Edward G. Seidensticker, vol. 1, p. 3.

20. Ichijō Kaneyoshi, "Sayo no nezame," in *Shinkō gunsho ruijū, kan* 21, p. 31. The translation is adapted from Steven D. Carter, *Regent Redux*, p. 182. Similar sentiments are found in "Shōdan chiyō," a guide to good government that Kaneyoshi wrote for Tomiko's son, the boy shogun Ashikaga Yoshihisa (*Gunsho ruijū, kan* 476, p. 193).

21. For a more detailed account of the dispute between the two Hatakeyama factions, see Varley, *Ōnin War*, pp. 86–96.

22. The name Ōnin is taken from the reign-name (*nengō*) used in 1467/1468. However, this reign-name was not adopted until the third month, and the fighting began two months earlier in what was the second year of Bunshō. The fighting also continued well beyond the end of the Ōnin era, but the name Ōnin no ran is used for the entire war.

23. For other dates that have been given for the commencement of hostilities, see Nagashima Fukutarō, *Ōnin no ran*, pp. 1–2.

Chapter 4

1. For the designations "eastern" and "western," see Nagahara Keiji, *Gekokujō no jidai*, p. 264. The headquarters of the Hosokawa forces were at the Muromachi *bakufu*, and they had encampments (*jin*) at Shōkoku-ji and at Hosokawa Katsumoto's mansion in Kitakōji-machi. The Yamana forces had their encampment in the area of Yamana Sōzen's mansion to the west. This gave rise to the

place-name Nishijin (West Camp) and to the custom of referring to the Hosokawa as the Eastern Army and the Yamana as the Western Army. Nagashima Fukutarō noted that the common interpretation of "Eastern" and "Western" as signifying east and west of the Palace of Flowers was mistaken (*Ōnin no ran*, p. 3).

2. Shimura Kunihiro, *Ōnin ki*, p. 266, in H. Paul Varley, *The Ōnin War*, p. 169.

3. "Ōnin bekki," in *Shinkō gunsho ruijū*, *kan* 376, p. 342. Jiken was the uncle of Hosokawa Katsumoto.

4. Varley, *Ōnin War*, p. 132. Varley cautiously accepts the figures given in *Ōnin ki* for the strength of the Hosokawa and Yamana forces but adds that this chronicle is not always reliable, that the number of soldiers involved in the fighting of this time was often exaggerated.

5. Varley, *Ōnin War*, p. 268. The term *kangun*, used of the Eastern Army, referred to troops fighting on the side of the emperor. The opponents, by definition, were rebels.

6. "Ōnin bekki," p. 346.

7. Ikkyū's reverence for the emperor may have stemmed from his birth: he was a son of Emperor Go-Komatsu.

8. Quoted in Hirano Sōjō, *Kyōunshū zenshaku*, vol. 1, p. 299. A contrast is being made between the general desolation and the palaces of the emperor and shogun, which remain unscathed. The emperor sent an envoy to halt the fighting between Shiba Yoshikado and Hatakeyama Yoshitsugu at the Shōkoku-ji. Although the intercession brought about a cease-fire, Ikkyū's joy was premature.

9. Quoted in Hirano, *Kyōunshū zenshaku*, vol. 1, p. 305.

10. Quoted in "Ōnin bekki," p. 355.

11. Quoted in Donald Keene, *Travelers of a Hundred Ages*, p. 95.

12. Haga Kōshirō, *Higashiyama bunka*, p. 12.

13. Ibid., p. 13.

14. The Bunmei era lasted from 1469 to 1486. The date of the poem is unknown, but presumably it was composed early in the era. The poem was evidently written on a day in late spring; plants and flowers that should have been seen in early spring have only now appeared, but even they seem autumnal and cheerless.

15. Yamagishi Tokuhei, ed., *Gozan bungaku shū, Edo kanshi shū*, pp. 154–55.

16. Ibid., p. 152.

17. Sasakawa Tanerō, *Higashiyama jidai no bunka*, pp. 25–26.

18. C. P. Fitzgerald, *China: A Short Cultural History*, p. 447. For more on Hui-tsung and his poetry, painting, and calligraphy, see Wen C. Fong and James C. Y. Watt, *Possessing the Past*, pp. 5–6, 164–68.

19. For Yoshimasa's calligraphy, see Matsubara Shigeru, ed., *Muromachi: Ashikaga Yoshimasa hyakushu waka*. Yoshimasa followed the Asukai school of calligraphy, founded by Asukai Masachika (1417–1470). Matsubara's book contains photographs of a hundred *waka* in Yoshimasa's handwriting. Komatsu Shigemi wrote of Yoshimasa's calligraphy that appropriately for one of the most cultivated persons of his time, it was "tranquil and overflowing with elegance" (*Nihon shodō jiten*, p. 7).

    The texts of the hundred *waka*, probably composed toward the close of Yoshimasa's life, are imbued with elegance, though they lack much individuality. The original manuscript, of great beauty, is about eighteen feet long. The last poem of the manuscript, not one of the hundred, humbly asks Reizei Tamehiro (1450–1526), a much younger man, to shed the "jeweled light" of his criticism on the "colorless hundred grasses" of the collection.

20. Sesshū studied painting in Kyoto under the equally famous Josetsu and Shūbun. See Haga, *Higashiyama bunka*, p. 63.

21. George B. Sansom, *A History of Japan*, vol. 2, *1334–1615*, p. 167.

22. Hung-wu sent envoys with the news not only to Japan but also to Annam, Champa, and Korea. See Wang Yi-T'ung, *Official Relations Between China and Japan, 1368–1549*, p. 10.

23. The pirates were known to the Chinese as *pa-fan*, their reading of the name of the god Hachiman, whose banners were displayed on the pirate ships. The Chinese also referred to them as *wakō* (*wo-k'ou*), meaning "Japanese bandits."

24. Quoted in Wang, *Official Relations*, p. 10.

25. Ibid., p. 11.

26. For an excellent summary of relations between the Chinese and Japanese courts at this time, see Sansom, *History of Japan*, vol. 2, pp. 168–69.

27. Quoted in Wang, *Official Relations*, p. 22.

28. Sansom, *History of Japan*, vol. 2, p. 170.

29. Minamoto was the Buddhist name that Yoshimitsu took in 1395.

30. Quoted in Wang, *Official Relations*, p. 22. The words "love of your ruler" refer, of course, to Yoshimitsu's love of the emperor of China, his superior.

31. Sansom, *History of Japan*, vol. 2, p. 172.

32. See, for example, Yoshimitsu's letter of 1403, translated in part in Wang, *Official Relations*, p. 24.

33. Sansom, *History of Japan*, vol. 2, p. 173.

34. Wang, *Official Relations*, p. 3.

35. Ibid., p. 64.

36. For a discussion of the attempts to define the limits of the Higashiyama era, see Yokoi Kiyoshi, *Higashiyama bunka*, pp. 17–21. Strictly speaking, the period lasted only from the time Yoshimasa started construction of his mountain retreat in 1483 until his death in 1490, but just as "Genroku" is used for a much longer period of culture than the years when it was the *nengō*, "Higashiyama" has been used to designate a large part of Yoshimasa's life.

Chapter 5

1. Morita Kyōji, *Ashikaga Yoshimasa no kenkyū*, pp. 112–13. The construction of the new Hana no gosho began just one month after the completion of the Karasumaru Palace. Muromachi-dono was a more formal way of referring to the same building.

2. For example, criticism of Yoshimasa's extravagance was expressed in *Hekizan nichiroku*, the diary of the monk Unsen Taikyoku.

3. Morita, *Ashikaga Yoshimasa*, p. 114.

4. For the account in Taikyoku's *Hekizan nichiroku*, see Morita, *Ashikaga Yoshimasa*, p. 114.

5. Yoshida Kenkō, *Tsurezuregusa*, 139 *dan*, in *Essays in Idleness*, trans. Donald Keene, p. 126.

6. For excerpts from contemporary diaries that describe the fire, see Morita, *Ashikaga Yoshimasa*, pp. 115–16. There are minor contradictions in the different accounts, as Morita points out.

7. Morita, *Ashikaga Yoshimasa*, p. 215; Haga Kōshirō, *Higashiyama bunka no kenkyū*, p. 418. For Kaneyoshi's "Shōdan chiyō," see *Gunsho ruijū, ken* 476, p. 193.

8. Officers (*hōkōshū*) who supported Yoshihisa and were eager to see the establishment of a new administration under Yoshihisa's control clashed with the supporters of Yoshimasa, who continued to take orders only from him. See Kawai Masaharu, *Ashikaga Yoshimasa*, p. 140.

9. Kawai, *Ashikaga Yoshimasa*, p. 140. The escape was to take place in the fifth month of 1480.

10. This rumor, recorded originally in *Daijōin jisha zōjiki*, is quoted in Kawai, *Ashikaga Yoshimasa*, p. 140. The lady in question was the daughter of Tokudaiji Kimiari.

11. It was on the twentieth day of the tenth month (November 12). For a quotation from the diary *Gohōkōin Masaie ki*, see Morita, *Ashikaga Yoshimasa*, p. 119.

12. Yokoi Kiyoshi, *Higashiyama bunka*, p. 139.

13. A "forbidden direction" was one where a god known as a *nakagami* resided. In order not to provoke his wrath by traveling in that direction, people were obliged to spend one night in a lucky direction. As we know from *The Tale of Genji* and other works of literature, the avoidance of an unlucky direction could provide a pretext for spending the night at some lady's house. For Yoshimasa's visit, chronicled in *Nagaoki Sukune ki* for this day, see Morita, *Ashikaga Yoshimasa*, p. 120.

14. For the names and functions of these buildings, see Yokoi, *Higashiyama bunka*, pp. 146–48.

15. Kurokawa Naonori, "Higashiyama sansō no zōei to sono haikei," in *Chūsei no kenryoku to minshū*, ed. Nihonshi kenkyūkai shiryō kenkyūbu kai, p. 242.

16. This theory, first given in *Daijōin jisha zōjiki*, is quoted in Kawai, *Ashikaga Yoshimasa*, p. 141; and Yokoi, *Higashiyama bunka*, p. 155.

17. Haga Kōshirō, *Higashiyama bunka*, p. 80. *Rinzairoku* was the Japanese name for the record of the sayings of the Chinese Zen priest Lin-chi I-hsüan (d. 867), the founder of the Rinzai sect.

18. Quoted in Haga, *Higashiyama bunka*, p. 79. See also Morita, *Ashikaga Yoshimasa*, p. 215. Morita cites a text that describes Yoshimasa on his deathbed receiving rites administered by a Jōdo priest.

19. Morita, *Ashikaga Yoshimasa*, p. 215. Haga gives an even fuller interpretation: "A person in the East, praying to Amida, seeks to be born in the West" (*Higashiyama bunka*, p. 72). The reference in both cases is to the Pure Land in the West, where those who call on Amida's help will be reborn.

20. Quoted in Kawai, *Ashikaga Yoshimasa*, p. 147.

21. Donald Keene, *Seeds in the Heart*, pp. 1079–80.

22. Haga, *Higashiyama bunka*, p. 153.

23. Quoted in ibid., p. 148. See also Morita, *Ashikaga Yoshimasa*, p. 178.

24. Quoted in Haga, *Higashiyama bunka*, p. 148. "Waiting for the Moon" is the name of the hill behind the Ginkaku-ji. The sinking of the moon in the sky suggests that his own life is coming to an end.

Chapter 6

1. *Shōji* are mentioned in old works of literature, but they were actually what are now called *fusuma*, sliding doors used to separate rooms, and not paper windows that admit light from the outside.

2. The name of the *chashitsu* was derived from the word *dōjin*, a Buddhist term whose expanded meaning is "under Amida all men are equal." The name was selected by Yoshimasa from several proposed by Ōsen Keisan. See Miyagami Shigetaka, "Ashikaga shōgun tei no kenchiku bunka," in *Kinkaku-ji, Ginkaku-ji*, ed. Shibata Akisuke, p. 122.

3. Miyagami, "Ashikaga shōgun," p. 114.

4. For the Ten Monks, see Morita Kyōji, *Ashikaga Yoshimasa no kenkyū*, p. 131. The theme was derived from the commentary to the *Kanmuryōju bukkyō* by Zendō (Shan Tao), an Amidist sutra of the T'ang period. The text states that "on the second night they saw Amida Buddha, his body pure gold, sitting on a golden lotus blossom under a jeweled tree. Ten monks sat on all sides of him, each one under a jeweled tree."

5. Quoted in Miyagami, "Ashikaga shōgun," p. 114.

6. *Dōbōshū* were men who dealt with the personal affairs of the Ashikaga shoguns, including the supervision of their collections of art. They took names ending with -ami, following the practice common among priests of the Jishū sect of Buddhism, though

they were not necessarily believers of that sect. For more on the *dōbōshū*, see Pierre François Souyri, *The World Turned Upside Down*, pp. 173–74.

7. Kawai Masaharu, *Ashikaga Yoshimasa*, p. 154. Kawai relates how, when Yoshimasa went with Kisen Shūshō to Shōkoku-ji, they were shown a triptych, said to be by Mu Ch'i, that had been donated to the monastery by Ashikaga Yoshimochi. Kisen believed that all three paintings were by Mu Ch'i, but Yoshimasa insisted that the middle painting, of Hotei, could not be by Mu Ch'i. The old priests were quite sure that the middle painting was also a genuine Mu Ch'i, but Yoshimasa dismissed their protests with a smile. Later, when Sōami and others examined the painting, they discovered that the date (given in cyclical characters) was an impossibility and that the painting itself must therefore be a fake.

8. Tanaka Hidemichi, *Nihon bijutsu zenshi*, p. 228.

9. Haga Kōshirō has written of a work, said to be "representative" of Shūbun, that it shows nothing more than competence in imitating the Northern Sung style, lacking depth (*Higashiyama bunka*, p. 61). Tanaka complains of the weakness of Shūbun's compositions (*Nihon bijutsu zenshi*, p. 232). Other critics have been more favorable, and some insist that Shūbun surpassed the Chinese masters whose works had originally inspired him.

10. It is not known whether Sesshū actually painted such a picture, but the account indirectly indicates the esteem in which Sesshū's art was held by the Chinese.

11. For Sesshū's reminiscence, see Haga, *Higashiyama bunka*, p. 63.

12. Yokoi Kiyoshi, *Higashiyama bunka*, p. 174. Masanobu, unusually for a painter of this time, had not entered Buddhist orders.

13. For more on this portrait of Ikkyū, see Donald Keene, *Landscapes and Portraits*, pp. 226–41.

Chapter 7

1. For a diagram of the reconstructed *tsunenogosho*, see Miyagami Shigetaka, "Ashikaga shōgun tei no kenchiku bunka," in *Kinkaku-ji, Ginkaku-ji*, ed. Shibata Akisuke, p. 118.

2. In turn, the *tsunenogosho* at the Higashiyama retreat served as the

model for the residential palace that Oda Nobunaga built at Azuchi from 1576 to 1579.

3. Yokoi Kiyoshi gives the number of laborers supplied by different donors (*Higashiyama bunka*, pp. 149–50).

4. For the plan of the *kaisho*, see Miyagami, "Ashikaga shōgun," p. 118.

5. Morita Kyōji, *Ashikaga Yoshimasa*, p. 127.

6. Yokoi has pointed out that even after Yoshimasa's death, none of the buildings was converted for public use (*Higashiyama bunka*, pp. 147–48).

7. Quoted in Morita, *Ashikaga Yoshimasa*, pp. 187–88. The manuscript includes what seem to be two false starts by Yoshimasa on his *waka* of reply.

8. Quoted (without attribution) in Sasakawa Tanerō, *Higashiyama jidai no bunka*, p. 36.

9. Haga Kōshirō, *Higashiyama bunka*, p. 44. Haga gives as the three great periods of *kanshi*: (1) the early Heian period, (2) the period from the Nanboku-chō to the middle Muromachi era, and (3) the middle Edo period. He argues, however, that although the *kanshi* and *kanbun* of the early Heian period maintained a lofty tone, the content was vacuous. Again, although the *kanshi* of the middle Edo period closely reflected the feelings of the poets, they were conventional, and the Japanese odor (*washū*) was strong. The Gozan poets, in contrast, maintained a lofty tone, and their poems belonged so genuinely to the mainstream of Chinese poetry as to astonish poets in China.

10. Quoted in Donald Keene, *World Within Walls*, p. 14. This example is actually from a later period, but it is typical of the short *renga*.

11. Quoted in Donald Keene, *Seeds in the Heart*, p. 956.

12. Quoted in Kidō Saizō and Imoto Nōichi, *Rengaron shū, hairon shū*, pp. 162–63, in Keene, *Seeds in the Heart*, p. 949.

13. Haga, *Higashiyama bunka*, p. 202.

14. Ibid., p. 205.

15. For a description of the occasion, derived from *Inryōken nichiroku*, see Sasakawa, *Higashiyama jidai no bunka*, p. 69.

16. Haga Kōshirō, *Chūsei zenrin no gakumon oyobi bungaku ni kansuru kenkyū*, p. 407. Haga is referring to professional Zen priests, as opposed to those who (like Yoshimasa) "left the world" to become

priests but did not observe monastic vows. Zen priests also took part in composing *wakan renga*. Wakan renga (also called *kanwa renga*) consisted of the alternation of verses in Japanese and Chinese. For a discussion of *wakan renga*, see *Nose Asaji chosakushū*, vol. 5, pp. 108–54.

17. Quoted in Morita, *Ashikaga Yoshimasa*, p. 180.

Chapter 8

1. Yamane Yūzō, *Kadōshi kenkyū*, p. 27.
2. Ibid., pp. 29–30.
3. Ibid., pp. 175–76.
4. *Inryōken nichiroku* is the diary of the chief monk of the Inryōken, a cloister within the Rokuon-in, a subtemple of the Shōkoku-ji. The earlier part was written by Kikei Shinzui, but the section from 1484 to 1493, the source of this quotation, was written by Kisen Shūshō (1424–1493).
5. Kawai Masaharu, *Ashikaga Yoshimasa*, p. 175.
6. Haga Kōshirō, *Higashiyama bunka no kenkyū*, p. 639.
7. Haga mentions Toragiku, a *kawaramono* whose talents as a gardener were recognized by Ashikaga Yoshinori in 1436 (*Higashiyama bunka no kenkyū*, p. 641).
8. Yoshinaga Yoshinobu, *Nihon no teien*, p. 168.
9. A *hiki* was a unit of currency, worth at various times ten to twenty-five *mon*, a copper coin.
10. Haga, *Higashiyama bunka no kenkyū*, p. 643. Some scholars believe that Kan'ami and Zeami, the creators of the art of nō, also were *kawaramono*, as were many other entertainers.
11. Haga, *Higashiyama bunka no kenkyū*, p. 646.
12. Quoted in Yokoi Kiyoshi, *Higashiyama bunka*, pp. 179–80.
13. Ibid., p. 179. When constructing the garden at the Chūin of the Kōfuku-ji in 1471, Zen'ami received a guarantee of thirty *hiki* each day; two thousand *hiki* in gifts; eleven assistants, each of whom received twenty *hiki* a day; and five hundred *hiki* in gifts for the village association (*sōchū*).
14. In 1940 a new theory claimed that the architect of the gardens was Ekishi Shūshin, who, like Kikei Shinzui and Kisen Shūshō, was a

monk of the Inryōken cloister within the Shōkoku-ji, but Haga has convincingly disproved this theory (*Higashiyama bunka no kenkyū*, p. 663).

15. Sakonshirō, another *kawaramono* garden expert, was known as the second Zen'ami, but little is recorded about his activities except that he designed a garden for Kisen Shūshō.

16. Yoshinaga, *Nihon no teien*, p. 186.

17. Haga, *Higashiyama bunka no kenkyū*, p. 681.

18. Ibid., p. 685.

Chapter 9

1. Kumakura Isao, *Chanoyu no rekishi*, p. 23.

2. Ibid., p. 25.

3. Ibid., p. 32.

4. See the poem by Nishikoribe no Hikogimi, in Kojima Noriyuki, *Kaifūsō, bunka shūrei shū, honchō monzui*, p. 264.

5. Kumakura, *Chanoyu*, pp. 36–37.

6. Kumakura writes that contrary to the general belief that Yōsai brought seeds of the tea plant to Japan, he probably sent seedlings (*Chanoyu*, p. 40).

7. Quoted in Wm. Theodore de Bary, Donald Keene, George Tanabe, and Paul Varley, comps., *Sources of Japanese Tradition*, 2d ed., vol. 1, *From Earliest Times to 1600*, pp. 393–95. See also Kumakura, *Chanoyu*, pp. 41–42.

8. Quoted in de Bary et al., *Sources of Japanese Tradition*, vol. 1, p. 419. See also Kumakura, *Chanoyu*, p. 61.

9. For an account of the activities of *basara* devotees, see Pierre François Souyri, *The World Turned Upside Down*, pp. 108–9, 113.

10. Kumakura, *Chanoyu*, pp. 68–69.

11. Kuwata Tadachika, *Nihon sadō shi*, pp. 56–57. The term *chanoyu* is also found in an entry dated 1526 in *Sōchō shuki*. See *The Journal of Sōchō*, trans. H. Mack Horton, pp. 109, 279.

12. Quoted in Kuwata Tadachika, *Yamanoue Sōji ki no kenkyū*, pp. 37–38. See also Kuwata, *Nihon sadō shi*, p. 51.

13. Kuwata, *Nihon sadō shi*, p. 53. The mention of Mokuami occurs in an entry for Bunmei 2 *nen* (1470) in *Daijōin jisha zōjiki*.

14. Kuwata, *Yamanoue Sōji*, p. 39.

15. The name is also pronounced as Jukō.

16. de Bary et al., *Sources of Japanese Tradition*, vol. 1, p. 395.

17. Esperanza Ramirez-Christensen, *Heart's Flower: The Life and Poetry of Shinkei*, esp. pp. 95, 121, 195–96, 237.

18. Quoted in Kidō Saizō and Imoto Nōichi, *Rengaron shū, hairon shū*, p. 143.

19. *Yamanoue Sōji ki*, p. 97, quoted in Ramirez-Christensen, *Heart's Flower*, p. 195. Takeno Jōō (1502–1555) popularized the teachings relating to the tea ceremony of Murata Shukō and was the teacher of Sen no Rikyū. See Ramirez-Christensen, *Heart's Flower*, p. 426.

20. It is possible that Shukō, familiar with the tea bowls favored by Yoshimasa (in Chinese taste), found antipathetic the views of those who insisted on the superiority of simple, unadorned Bizen and Shigaraki wares and who rejected the elegance of Chinese bowls. That was why, criticizing those who advocated the exclusive use of Japanese wares, he insisted on combining the two. Only with Rikyū did *wamono* (Japanese pottery) come into general use in the tea ceremony.

21. Adapted from de Bary et al., *Sources of Japanese Tradition*, vol. 1, pp. 395–96. The quotation at the end is from the Daihan nehan Sutra. See Kumakura, *Chanoyu*, p. 112.

22. Murai Yasuhiko, "The Development of *Chanoyu* Before Rikyū," in *Tea in Japan*, ed. H. Paul Varley and Kumakura Isao, p. 24.

23. Quoted in Michael Cooper, *They Came to Japan*, p. 265.

Chapter 10

1. Yoshimasa's teacher of perfume blending was the celebrated Murata Shukō, and Yoshimasa himself was rated as one of the luminaries of this art. See Ōta Kiyoshi, *Kō to chanoyu*, p. 63. In 1465, when Yoshimasa visited Nara, he asked that the Shōsōin, the treasure-house at the Tōdai-ji, be opened. On this occasion, he cut off a piece of the *ranjatai*, a celebrated log of incense wood. His action was imitated in later years by Oda Nobunaga and Emperor Meiji. See Morita Kyōji, *Ashikaga Yoshimasa no kenkyū*, p. 208.

2. For Yoshimasa's frequent participation in sessions of *renga*, see

Morita, *Ashikaga Yoshimasa*, pp. 152, 156. Kawai Masaharu quotes Nōami, who said of the *hokku* that Yoshimasa supplied for a *renga* session held in 1466: "Lord Yoshimasa's *hokku* were always extraordinary" (*Ashikaga Yoshimasa*, p. 175). Nōami's praise was possibly colored by respect for his master, but at the very least, Yoshimasa was a skillful *renga* poet. Three hundred of his *waka* were collected in *Yoshimasa-kō shūō*. See Morita, *Ashikaga Yoshimasa*, pp. 160–88. Yoshimasa also sponsored *waka* poetry. In 1466 the *bakufu* provided funds to establish a *wakadokoro* in the residence of Asukai Masachika, who was entrusted with preparing a new imperial anthology. With the outbreak of the Ōnin War in the following year, the Asukai residence was consumed in flames, and the twenty-second anthology was never completed. See Haga Kōshirō, *Higashiyama bunka*, pp. 97–100.

3. Haga Kōshirō lists Yoshimasa's religious activities for one year, Kanshō 5 (1464) (*Higashiyama bunka no kenkyū*, pp. 395–99). On virtually every day, he visited the Shōkoku-ji or some other temple. He listened to sermons (most often on the Lotus Sutra), arranged for sutras to be copied, and participated in whenever rites were conducted at the *bakufu* palace. He also visited Shinto shrines and deeply venerated the Shinto gods. One gets the impression from Haga's chronology, based on *Inryōken nichiroku*, that Yoshimasa could not have had much time left for politics.

4. Quoted in Haga, *Higashiyama bunka no kenkyū*, p. 433. For the Zen rejection of "words and letters," see Wm. Theodore de Bary, Donald Keene, George Tanabe, and Paul Varley, comps., *Sources of Japanese Tradition*, 2d ed., vol. 1, *From Earliest Times to 1600*, p. 315: "If anyone says the Buddha's Zen exists in words, letters, or speech, then that person slanders the Buddha and slanders the dharma."

5. Haga, *Higashiyama bunka no kenkyū*, pp. 438–39.

6. Quoted in de Bary et al., *Sources of Japanese Tradition*, vol. 1, p. 218. See also Haga, *Higashiyama bunka no kenkyū*, p. 448.

7. For a good account of Rennyo in English, see Stanley Weinstein, "Rennyo and the Shinshū Revival," in *Japan in the Muromachi Age*, ed. John Whitney Hall and Toyoda Takeshi.

8. Quoted in Kasahara Kazuo, *Rennyo*, p. 133, in de Bary et al., *Sources of Japanese Tradition*, vol. 1, p. 228.

9. Arthur H. Thornhill III, *Six Circles, One Dewdrop*, p. 10.

10. Zeami, "Finding Gems and Gaining the Flower," in *On the Art of the Nō Drama: The Major Treatises of Zeami*, trans. J. Thomas Rimer and Yamazaki Masakazu. The attribution to Zeami of "Six Principles," a brief work on the relations of the art of the *waka* to nō, has been questioned.

11. On'ami was the last of the three generations of *Kan*'ami, Zeami, and *On*'ami. Zeami's name was traditionally pronounced as Seami until a scholar, noticing that the first syllables of the three names formed Kanzeon (Avalokiteshvara), concluded that the name should be pronounced as Zeami rather than Seami. The fact that Motoshige was given the name On'ami suggests that it was expected, at least before the birth of Motomasa, that he would be Zeami's successor. The first character in the name Motoshige is the same as in Motokiyo (Zeami's personal name) and in Motomasa (the name of Zeami's elder son), another indication that he was expected to succeed Zeami as head of the Kanze school. See Dōmoto Masaki, *Zeami*, p. 202.

12. The name Saburō (third son) also suggests that it was anticipated that he would be the "third generation" of masters of the Kanze school, after Kan'ami and Zeami. He received the name Motoshige at the time of his *genbuku*.

13. One recalls the similar situation in Yoshimasa's family: having despaired of having a son, he adopted his younger brother (Yoshimi) as his heir, only for his wife to give birth to a son (Yoshihisa).

14. Dōmoto, *Zeami*, p. 352.

15. This practice, known as *isshi sōden*, is still observed in various traditional arts.

16. For a table of attributions of plays to Zenchiku, see Nishino Haruo, "Zenchiku no nō," in *Iwanami kōza: Nō kyōgen*, vol. 3, pp. 207–9. Nishino divides the plays attributed to Zenchiku into four categories, ranging from the one play (*Bashō*) that is undoubtedly by him, through various degrees of reliability in attributions, down to the fourth category of plays that are only "possibly" by Zenchiku.

17. Thornhill, *Six Circles*, p. 19.
18. Yoshimasa saw both Zenchiku and On'ami perform at the Kasuga Shrine at the time of his visit there in 1465. See Kawatake Shigetoshi, *Nihon engeki zenshi*, p. 152.
19. Dōmoto, *Zeami*, p. 471.
20. Ibid., p. 536. Zeami would have been seventy-one by Western count.
21. Dōmoto, *Zeami*, p. 570.
22. Donald Keene, *Nō, the Classical Theatre of Japan*, p. 73. The *happi* with the dragonfly pattern is reproduced on p. 213. Another robe, a magnificent *chōken* (long-sleeved jacket), originally given to the Kongō school by Yoshimasa, has been rewoven in recent years and is shown on p. 214.
23. For Yoshimi's desertion to the Yamana, see H. Paul Varley, *The Ōnin War*, p. 188.

BIBLIOGRAPHY

Atsuta Kō. "Hino Tomiko kenkyū no mondaiten."
Rekishi kenkyū, no. 353, September 1990.

Berry, Mary Elizabeth. *The Culture of Civil War in Kyoto.*
Berkeley: University of California Press, 1994.

Carter, Steven D. *Literary Patronage in Late Medieval
Japan.* Ann Arbor: Center for Japanese Studies,
University of Michigan, 1993.

Carter, Steven D. *Regent Redux.* Ann Arbor: Center for
Japanese Studies, University of Michigan, 1996.

Cooper, Michael. *They Came to Japan.* London: Thames
& Hudson, 1965.

de Bary, Wm. Theodore, Donald Keene, George
Tanabe, and Paul Varley, comps. *Sources of Japanese Tradition.* Vol. 1, *From Earliest Times to 1600.* 2d
ed. New York: Columbia University Press, 2001.

Dōmoto Masaki. *Zeami.* Tokyo: Geki shobō, 1986.

Elison, George, and Bardwell L. Smith, eds. *Warlords,*

Artists, and Commoners. Honolulu: University of Hawai'i Press, 1981.

Fitzgerald, C. P. *China: A Short Cultural History.* New York: Appleton-Century, 1938.

Fong, Wen C., and James C. Y. Watt. *Possessing the Past.* New York: Metropolitan Museum of Art, 1996.

Futaki Ken'ichi. *Chūsei buke no sahō.* Tokyo: Yoshikawa kōbunkan, 1999.

Grossberg, Kenneth Alan. *Japan's Renaissance: The Politics of the Muromachi Bakufu.* Cambridge, Mass.: Harvard University Press, 1981.

Haga Kōshirō. *Chūsei zenrin no gakumon oyobi bungaku ni kansuru kenkyū.* Tokyo: Nihon gakujutsu shinkōkai, 1956.

Haga Kōshirō. *Higashiyama bunka.* Tokyo: Hanawa shobō, 1962.

Haga Kōshirō. *Higashiyama bunka no kenkyū.* Tokyo: Kawade shobō, 1945.

Haga Kōshirō. *Sanjōnishi Sanetaka.* Jinbutsu sōsho series. Tokyo: Yoshikawa kōbunkan, 1960.

Hall, John Whitney, and Jeffrey P. Mass. *Medieval Japan: Essays in Institutional History.* Stanford, Calif.: Stanford University Press, 1988.

Hall, John Whitney, and Toyoda Takeshi, eds. *Japan in the Muromachi Age.* Berkeley: University of California Press, 1977.

Hayashiya Tatsusaburō. *Kinsei no reimei.* Tokyo: Iwanami shoten, 1988.

Hayashiya Tatsusaburō. "Kyoto in the Muromachi Age." In *Japan in the Muromachi Age,* edited by John Whitney Hall and Toyoda Takeshi. Berkeley: University of California Press, 1977.

Hirano Sōjō. *Kyōunshū zenshaku.* Tokyo: Shunjūsha, 1976.

Ichijō Kaneyoshi. "Sayo no nezame." In *Shinkō gunsho ruijū, kan* 21. Tokyo: Naigai shoseki, 1930.

Ichijō Kaneyoshi. "Shōdan chiyō." In *Gunsho ruijū, kan* 476. Tokyo: Zoku gunsho ruijū kansei kai, 1931.

Imatani Akira. *Ashikaga shōgun ansatsu.* Tokyo: Shinjinbutsu ōrai sha, 1994.

Imatani Akira. *Nihon kokuō to domin.* Nihon no rekishi series. Tokyo: Shūseisha, 1992.

Imatani Akira. *Sengoku daimyō to minshū*. Tokyo: Fukutake shoten, 1992.

Itō Teiji. "The Development of Shoin-Style Architecture." In *Japan in the Muromachi Age*, edited by John Whitney Hall and Toyoda Takeshi. Berkeley: University of California Press, 1977.

Iwanami kōza: Nō kyōgen. Vol. 3. Tokyo: Iwanami shoten, 1987.

Kakitsu monogatari. Zoku gunsho ruijū series, *kan* 577. Tokyo: Zoku gunsho ruijū kansei kai, 1923.

Kamei Katsuichirō. *Muromachi geijutsu to minshū no kokoro*. Tokyo: Bungei shunjū sha, 1966.

Kasahara Kazuo. *Rennyo*. Jinbutsu sōsho series. Tokyo: Yoshikawa kōbunkan, 1961.

Kawai Masaharu. *Ashikaga Yoshimasa*. Tokyo: Shimizu shoin, 1972.

Kawatake Shigetoshi. *Nihon engeki zenshi*. Tokyo: Iwanami shoten, 1959.

Keene, Donald. *Landscapes and Portraits*. Tokyo: Kodansha International, 1971.

Keene, Donald. *Nō, the Classical Theatre of Japan*. Tokyo: Kodansha International, 1966.

Keene, Donald. *The Pleasures of Japanese Literature*. New York: Columbia University Press, 1988.

Keene, Donald. *Seeds in the Heart*. New York: Holt, 1993.

Keene, Donald. *Travelers of a Hundred Ages*. New York: Holt, 1989.

Keene, Donald. *World Within Walls*. New York: Holt, Rinehart and Winston, 1976.

Kidō Saizō and Imoto Nōichi. *Rengaron shū, hairon shū*. Nihon koten bungaku taikei series. Tokyo: Iwanami shoten, 1961.

Kobayashi Chigusa. *Ōnin no ran to Hino Tomiko*. Chūkō shinsho series. Tokyo: Chūō kōron sha, 1993.

Kojima Noriyuki. *Kaifūsō, bunka shūrei shū, honchō monzui*. Nihon koten bungaku taikei series. Tokyo: Iwanami shoten, 1964.

Komatsu Shigemi. *Nihon shodō jiten*. Tokyo: Nigensha, 1987.

Kumakura Isao. *Chanoyu no rekishi*. Tokyo: Asahi shinbunsha, 1990.

Kurokawa Naonori. "Higashiyama sansō no zōei to sono haikei." In *Chūsei no kenryoku to minshū*, edited by Nihonshi kenkyūkai shiryō kenkyūbu kai. Osaka: Sōgensha, 1970.

Kuwata Tadachika, ed. *Ashikaga shōgun retsuden*. Tokyo: Akita shoten, 1975.

Kuwata Tadachika. *Nihon sadō shi*. Tokyo: Kadokawa shoten, 1962.

Kuwata Tadachika. *Yamanoue Sōji ki no kenkyū*. Kyoto: Kawahara shoten, 1957.

Kyōto koseki kenkyūkai, ed. *Ginkaku-ji*. Kyoto, n.d. [Also issued as *Jishō-ji*]

Matsubara Shigeru, ed. *Muromachi: Ashikaga Yoshimasa hyakushu waka*. Tokyo: Nigensha, 1979.

Miyagami Shigetaka. "Ashikaga shōgun tei no kenchiku bunka." In *Kinkaku-ji, Ginkaku-ji*, edited by Shibata Akisuke. Nihon meikenchiku shashin senshū series. Tokyo: Shinchōsha, 1992.

Morita Kyōji. *Ashikaga Yoshimasa no kenkyū*. Osaka: Izumi shoin, 1993.

Moriya Takeshi. *Kyō no geinō*. Chūkō shinsho series. Tokyo: Chūō kōron sha, 1979.

Murai Yasuhiko. "The Development of *Chanoyu* Before Rikyū." In *Tea in Japan*, edited by H. Paul Varley and Kumakura Isao. Honolulu: University of Hawai'i Press, 1989.

Murai Yasuhiko. *Kinkaku to Ginkaku*. Asahi hyakka Nihon no rekishi series. Tokyo: Asahi shinbun sha, 1985.

Murasaki Shikibu. *The Tale of Genji*. Translated by Edward G. Seidensticker. New York: Knopf, 1976.

Nagahara Keiji. *Gekokujō no jidai*. Chūkō bunko series. Tokyo: Chūō kōron sha, 1974.

Nagashima Fukutarō. *Ōnin no ran*. Nihon rekishi shinsho series. Tokyo: Shibundō, 1968.

Nakamura Naokatsu. *Higashiyama-dono Yoshimasa shiden*. Kyoto: Kawahara shoten, 1970.

Nihonshi kenkyūkai shiryō kenkyūbu kai, ed. *Chūsei no kenryoku to minshū*. Osaka: Sōgensha, 1970.

Nishida Masayoshi. *Nihon no runessansu*. Tokyo: Hanawa shoten, 1977.

Nishino Haruo. "Zenchiku no nō." In *Iwanami kōza: Nō kyōgen*. Vol. 3. Tokyo: Iwanami shoten, 1987.

Nose Asaji chosakushū. Kyoto: Shibunkaku, 1981.

Ogawa Makoto. *Yamana Sōzen to Hosokawa Katsumoto*. Tokyo: Jinbutsu ōrai sha, 1966.

"Ōnin bekki." In *Shinkō gunsho ruijū, kan* 378. Tokyo: Naigai shoseki, 1936.

Ōno Isao. *Higashiyama bunka to minshū*. Tokyo: Hyōronsha, 1970.

Ōta Hirotarō. *Nihon kenchiku no tokushitsu*. Tokyo: Iwanami shoten, 1983.

Ōta Hirotarō. *Shoin-zukuri*. In *Nihon bijutsushi sōsho*, vol. 5. Tokyo: Tōkyō daigaku shuppankai, 1966.

Ōta Kiyoshi. *Kō to chanoyu*. Kyoto: Tankōsha, 2001.

Phillips, Quitman E. *The Practice of Painting in Japan, 1475–1500*. Stanford, Calif.: Stanford University Press, 2000.

Ramirez-Christiansen, Esperanza. *Heart's Flower: The Life and Poetry of Shinkei*. Stanford, Calif.: Stanford University Press, 1994.

Sansom, George B. *A History of Japan*. Vol. 2, *1334–1615*. Stanford, Calif.: Stanford University Press, 1961.

Sasakawa Tanerō. *Higashiyama jidai no bunka*. Osaka: Sōgensha, 1943.

Shibata Akisuke, ed. *Kinkaku-ji, Ginkaku-ji*. Nihon meikenchiku shashin senshū series. Tokyo: Shinchōsha, 1992.

Shimura Kunihiro. *Ōnin ki*. Tokyo: Benseisha, 1994.

"Shinsen chōroku kanshō." In *Gunsho ruijū, kan* 375. Tokyo: Zoku gunsho ruijū kansei kai, 1929.

Sōchō. *The Journal of Sōchō*. Translated and annotated by H. Mack Horton. Stanford, Calif.: Stanford University Press, 2002.

Souyri, Pierre François. *The World Turned Upside Down*. New York: Columbia University Press, 2001.

Suzuki Ryōichi. *Daijōin jisha zōjiki*. Tokyo: Soshiete, 1983.

Takahashi Osamu. "Hino (Uramatsu) Shigeko ni kansuru ikkōsatsu." *Kokushigaku*, no. 137, 1989.

Takenaka Iku and Murakami Jikai. *Kinkaku-ji, Ginkaku-ji*. Furudera junrei Kyōto series. Kyoto: Tankōsha, 1977.

Tanaka Hidemichi. *Nihon bijutsu zenshi*. Tokyo: Kōdansha, 1995.

Tanaka Yoshinari. *Ashikaga jidai shi*. Kōdansha gakujutsu bunko series. Tokyo: Kōdansha, 1979.

Thornhill, Arthur H., III. *Six Circles, One Dewdrop: The Religio-Aesthetic World of Komparu Zenchiku*. Princeton, N.J.: Princeton University Press, 1993.

Unsen Taikyoku. *Hekizan nichiroku*. Edited by Takeuchi Rizō. Kyoto: Rinsen shoten, 1982.

Varley, H. Paul. *Imperial Restoration in Medieval Japan*. New York: Columbia University Press, 1971.

Varley, H. Paul. *The Ōnin War*. New York: Columbia University Press, 1967.

Varley, H. Paul, and George Elison. "The Culture of Tea: From Its Origins to Sen no Rikyū." In *Warlords, Artists, and Commoners*, edited by George Elison and Bardwell L. Smith. Honolulu: University of Hawai'i Press, 1981.

Varley, H. Paul, and Kumakura Isao, eds. *Tea in Japan*. Honolulu: University of Hawai'i Press, 1989.

Wakita Haruko. *Muromachi jidai*. Chūkō shinsho series. Tokyo: Chūō kōron sha, 1985.

Wang Yi-T'ung. *Official Relations Between China and Japan, 1368–1549*. Cambridge, Mass.: Harvard University Press, 1953.

Watson, Burton, trans. *Records of the Grand Historian of China*. New York: Columbia University Press, 1961.

Weinstein, Stanley. "Rennyo and the Shinshū Revival." In *Japan in the Muromachi Age*, edited by John Whitney Hall and Toyoda Takeshi. Berkeley: University of California Press, 1977.

Yamagishi Tokuhei, ed. *Gozan bungaku shū, Edo kanshi shū*. Nihon koten bungaku taikei series. Tokyo: Iwanami shoten, 1966.

Yamane Yūzō. *Kadōshi kenkyū*. Tokyo: Chūō kōron bijutsu shuppan, 1996.

Yokoi Kiyoshi. *Chūsei wo ikita hitobito*. Fukutake bunko series. Tokyo: Fukutake shoten, 1991.

Yokoi Kiyoshi. *Higashiyama bunka*. Heibonsha raiburarii series. Tokyo: Heibonsha, 1994.

Yokoi Kiyoshi. *Kanmon gyōki*. Tokyo: Soshiete, 1979.

Yoshida Kenkō. *Essays in Idleness*. Translated by Donald Keene. New York: Columbia University Press, 1967.

Yoshimi Kaneko. *Hino Tomiko no subete*. Tokyo: Shin jinbutsu ōrai sha, 1994.

Yoshimura Teiji. *Hino Tomiko*. Chūkō shinsho series. Tokyo: Chūō kōron sha, 1985.

Yoshinaga Yoshinobu. *Nihon no teien*. Tokyo: Shibundō, 1968.

Zeami. *On the Art of the Nō Drama: The Major Treatises of Zeami*. Translated by J. Thomas Rimer and Yamazaki Masakazu. Princeton, N.J.: Princeton University Press, 1984.